ASIA SMALL AND MEDIUM-SIZED ENTERPRISE MONITOR 2020

VOLUME III—THEMATIC CHAPTER: FINTECH LOANS TO TRICYCLE DRIVERS IN THE PHILIPPINES

NOVEMBER 2020

ADB

ASIAN DEVELOPMENT BANK

ISBN 978-92-9262-486-6 (print); 978-92-9262-487-3 (electronic); 978-92-9262-488-0 (ebook)
Publication Stock No. TCS200331-2
DOI: http://dx.doi.org/10.22617/TCS200331-2

The views expressed in this publication are those of the authors and do not necessarily reflect the views and policies of the Asian Development Bank (ADB) or its Board of Governors or the governments they represent.

ADB does not guarantee the accuracy of the data included in this publication and accepts no responsibility for any consequence of their use. The mention of specific companies or products of manufacturers does not imply that they are endorsed or recommended by ADB in preference to others of a similar nature that are not mentioned.

By making any designation of or reference to a particular territory or geographic area, or by using the term "country" in this document, ADB does not intend to make any judgments as to the legal or other status of any territory or area.

Please contact pubsmarketing@adb.org if you have questions or comments with respect to content, or if you wish to obtain copyright permission for your intended use that does not fall within these terms, or for permission to use the ADB logo.

Corrigenda to ADB publications may be found at http://www.adb.org/publications/corrigenda.

Notes:
In this publication, "$" refers to United States dollars unless otherwise stated.
ADB recognizes "Hong Kong" as Hong Kong, China.

Cover design by Claudette Rodrigo.

Printed on recycled paper

Contents

Tables and Figures

Foreword

Micro, small, and medium-sized enterprises (MSMEs) play a crucial role in most economies. They are particularly important in developing countries where firm size distribution is generally skewed toward smaller enterprises. They generate the majority of business opportunities and create numerous jobs worldwide. In Southeast Asia, MSMEs accounted for an average 97% of all enterprises, 69% of the total workforce, and 41% of a country's gross domestic product during 2010–2019. This suggests that the region's robust growth over the past decade was largely underpinned by MSMEs. Hence, MSME development is a national policy priority in promoting inclusive growth. However, limited access to formal financial services ranks first as a barrier impeding their business development.

This report is the thematic chapter of the Asia Small and Medium-Sized Enterprise Monitor (ASM) 2020. It explores selected country best practices related to MSME development by using an impact evaluation approach—an approach that assesses how an intervention affects particular outcomes compared with non-intervention. This is a useful analytical tool to evaluate the impact of policy interventions on MSME development in developing member countries of the Asian Development Bank (ADB). Volume III of the 2020 edition focuses on financial technology (fintech) loans to self-employed tricycle drivers in the Philippines. It examines how fintech affects their welfare and contributes to regional economic development.

The ADB team collaborated with Japan's fintech solution provider Global Mobility Service and with the tricycle operators and drivers' associations in the Philippines to complete the baseline survey in December 2019. The study was financed by the Japan Fund for Poverty Reduction as part of the ASM project. We would like to express our gratitude for their valuable contributions to this study.

This Volume III of ASM 2020 provides a benchmark analysis on the role financing constraints play in determining firm growth. It analyzes the specific fintech-based loan structure and its impact on Filipino tricycle drivers—in their lives and in business. The coronavirus disease (COVID-19) crisis is driving a more rapid shift toward digital transactions across all businesses. Smaller firms and the self-employed—such as tricycle drivers—are not exempted from this trend, as their business generally requires personal contact. The survey results offer some insight on financing models for the self-employed in the post-COVID-19 era. We hope this report contributes to policy discussions on support measures for the self-employed or sole proprietorships under the emerging "new normal."

Yasuyuki Sawada
Chief Economist and Director General
Economic Research and Regional Cooperation Department
Asian Development Bank

Acknowledgments

The Asia Small and Medium-Sized Enterprise Monitor (ASM) Volume III was prepared by a thematic study sub-team of the ASM. It comprises the subject experts as authors. The thematic study was led by Shigehiro Shinozaki, senior economist, Economic Research and Regional Cooperation Department (ERCD), Asian Development Bank (ADB). The work was supervised by Joseph Ernest Zveglich Jr., deputy chief economist. It benefited from the advice and inputs from Yasuyuki Sawada, chief economist and director general of ERCD; and Takashi Yamano, senior economist of the Economic Analysis and Operational Support Division.

The study was conducted in cooperation with Japan's fintech solution provider Global Mobility Service (GMS) and the tricycle operators and drivers' associations (TODAs) of the Philippines, with special thanks to Tokushi Nakashima, president and chief executive officer of GMS, and Kazumasa Nakashima, chief executive officer of GMS Philippines, for their support to the study. The baseline survey was conducted by the Manila-based consulting firm Orient Integrated Development Consultants (OIDCI) during November–December 2019. The study was funded by the Japan Fund for Poverty Reduction as co-financing partner to the ASM. Administrative support was provided by Richard Supangan and Maria Frederika Bautista.

Author Profiles

Hyuncheol Bryant Kim is an associate professor in the Economics Department at Hong Kong University of Science and Technology, and an assistant professor in the Department of Policy Analysis and Management at Cornell University, United States. He is an applied empirical micro-economist focusing on causal impacts of policy interventions in health and education sectors through large-scale data analysis and social experiment. The main goal of his research is to understand the fundamental relationship between human capital investment and individual and societal well-being in Africa and Asia. He received a master's degree from Yonsei University, the Republic of Korea, and a doctor of philosophy (PhD) degree in economics from Columbia University. His research is published in leading journals such as *Science, Review of Economics and Statistics, Journal of Public Economics, Journal of Health Economics,* and other international journals.

Syngjoo Choi is a professor of economics at Seoul National University, Republic of Korea, and is co-director of the Center for Experimental and Behavioral Social Science at Seoul National University. Previously, he worked as an assistant and (tenured) associate professor at University College London, United Kingdom, and served on the Editorial Board of *the Review of Economic Studies*. He received his PhD in Economics from New York University in 2006. His research interests include experimental economics and behavioral economics with particular emphasis on large-scale data collection with experimental methods to measure and identify policy impacts. His research has been published in *Science, American Economic Review, Journal of the European Economic Association,* and other international journals.

Shigehiro Shinozaki is a senior economist at ERCD, ADB. He supports ADB's developing member countries to improve micro, small, and medium-sized enterprise (MSME) access to finance through technical assistance projects. His advisory and research expertise includes policy issues in MSME development, inclusive finance, and financial sector development especially in developing Asia. Prior to joining ADB, he held various expert positions, including as special officer for development finance at Japan's Ministry of Finance, an advisor to the Indonesian Capital Market and Financial Institution Supervisory Agency (Bapepam-LK) as Japan International Cooperation Agency (JICA) expert, and as administrator of the Directorate for Financial and Enterprise Affairs at the Organisation for Economic Co-operation and Development (OECD). He holds a PhD in international studies from Waseda University in Japan and a master's degree in business administration from École Nationale des Ponts et Chaussées in France.

Siho Park is a PhD student at University of Illinois at Urbana-Champaign, with an interest in development and behavioral economics. He is currently working as a research assistant in impact evaluation studies in the Philippines and Tonga. He obtained a master's degree in economics from the Chinese University of Hong Kong.

Abbreviations

ADB	—	Asian Development Bank
CCEI	—	Critical Cost Efficiency Index
COVID-19	—	coronavirus disease
ERCD	—	Economic Research and Regional Cooperation Department
GARP	—	Generalized Axiom of Revealed Preference
GMS	—	Global Mobility Service
IoT	—	Internet of Things
MSME	—	micro, small, and medium-sized enterprise
OIDCI	—	Orient Integrated Development Consultants
TODA	—	tricycle operators and drivers' association

Executive Summary

Micro, small, and medium-sized enterprises (MSMEs) play a crucial role in most economies. They are particularly important in developing countries where firm size distribution is generally skewed to smaller enterprises. They generate the majority of business opportunities and create numerous jobs worldwide. In Southeast Asia, MSMEs accounted for an average 97% of all enterprises, 69% of the total workforce, and 41% of a country's gross domestic product (GDP) during 2010–2019 (ADB, 2020a). In the Philippines, 99.5% of all enterprises are MSMEs, accounting for 63.2% of total employment in 2018, the latest year with available data. This suggests that Southeast Asia's robust growth over the past decade was largely underpinned by MSMEs. The Philippine economy also exemplifies this trend. Hence, MSME development is a national policy priority in promoting inclusive growth. Among the list of factors impeding MSME development, limited access to formal financial services ranks first. MSMEs are inherently constrained in their ability to access credit compared with larger firms. This is largely due to their small size, absence of collateral, and the problem of asymmetric information between lenders and borrowers.

This report focuses on the role financing constraints play in determining firm growth. It examines financial technology (fintech)-based loans and their impact on Philippine self-employed tricycle drivers and the impact on their lives and businesses. The self-employed, sole proprietorships, and family-run or home businesses are an important part of MSME development discussions—together with the informal business sector. However, MSME statistics in developing Asia generally rely on registered enterprises and national census surveys, where actual state of informal (or unregistered) MSMEs are not well tracked nationally.

This study examines the fintech loan program for tricycle drivers in the Philippines, marketed by Japan's fintech solution provider Global Mobility Service (GMS). The tricycle is a three-wheel vehicle popularly utilized by people in developing Asia in short range transportation. It is mostly comprised of a motorcycle with a sidecar; although there are increasingly single-unit tricycles as well, with a few battery-powered. The loan program covered in this report adopts the recent breakthrough in Internet of Things (IoT) technology to alleviate moral hazard and imperfect loan repayment enforcement. The key innovation is that tricycle drivers become able to access auto-financing without collateral by using a remote control IoT device that is able to safely deactivate the motorcycle engine should the driver fail to repay on time—a clear incentive to make loan payments on schedule. With this IoT device, the fintech firm (lender) can remotely access various tricycle data, such as global positioning system (GPS) coordinates, distance traveled, time traveled, battery information, speed, and engine oil level. It allows constant monitoring of borrowers and hence significantly reduces monitoring costs. This information gives lenders the ability to limit any information disadvantage regarding working behavior—and hence helps overcome moral hazard. This report aims to estimate the impact of the new financing scheme on a driver's well-being and more generally on regional economic development.

The study was conducted in collaboration with GMS and with the cooperation of the tricycle operators and drivers' associations (TODAs) in the Philippines. The baseline survey was conducted by the Manila-based consulting firm Orient Integrated Development Consultants (OIDCI) during November–December 2019. The survey received responses from 2,487 randomly sampled tricycle drivers, consisting of two main groups: (i) conventional drivers from the City of Manila or Quezon City, and (ii) fintech drivers dispersed in different cities across Metropolitan Manila, or the National Capital Region (NCR).

Comparing the fintech and conventional drivers, the study found that fintech drivers have more risk appetite, more rationalized working hours, and earn much higher incomes than conventional drivers. They have relatively better access to financing sources and have good financial plans and goals, but face large obligations to loan repayments. Debit card bank account ownership is higher among fintech drivers—credit card and mobile banking as well as online shopping are rare. They have a savings habit, but mostly use cash kept at home and informal savings groups; few use formal financial institutions to save. The study's regression analysis indicated that fintech loans stimulate driver work habits—with more work days per week, higher overall income, improved money management with financial goals, and create a savings habit for business operations. While the burden of loan repayments reduces the incentive to borrow for non-tricycle purposes, fintech loans should drive more people to open bank accounts. Overall, the survey findings suggest that using fintech loans improves living standards and the social welfare of tricycle drivers—and could potentially support the development of local economies by enhancing financial inclusion.

The key findings of the baseline tricycle driver survey hold several implications about financing models for the self-employed. As the survey was conducted in 2019, it does not reflect how the coronavirus disease (COVID-19) impacted fintech loans to tricycle drivers. Nonetheless, the results emphasize the importance of fintech for the self-employed in adapting to the post-COVID-19 "new normal."

COVID-19 triggered a shift of MSME business models—from conventional ways requiring personal contact to more contactless digital transactions. The tricycle driving industry operates on a community-based relationship market across the Philippines—and thus may not naturally or easily transform to digital transactions due to its form of business. However, mobile-based ride-hailing services modelled on the Singapore-based Grab and the Philippine-based Angkas, for example, may help make new digital operations attractive for the tricycle driving industry post-COVID-19. At the very least, they will need to ensure the safety of their customers to retain business under the new normal—by placing partitions in the customer compartment and enforcing face mask and/or face shield mandates. To customize their tricycles to protect customers from the virus, they may require additional funding. But the popular community-based lending and/or informal financing used are always accompanied by physical contact. Given the high penetration of smartphone use among tricycle drivers, it offers a good opportunity to promote fintech lending or other digital financial services—including savings and insurance for drivers.

Financial education or financial literacy training—including digital finance—is critical for tricycle drivers to access more, new, and better financial tools. They will need the appropriate knowledge and understanding of the benefits these tools provide. Given that most tricycle drivers are male, financial literacy training for wives or female partners is essential to help promote fintech loans or other digital finance opportunities—as women in the Philippines generally hold certain decision-making power over household budgets. This financial education will also cultivate a new customer base or risk-takers for the fintech loan and digital finance industry.

1. Introduction

Micro, small, and medium-sized enterprises (MSMEs) play a crucial role in most economies. They are particularly important to developing countries where firm size distribution is generally skewed to smaller enterprises. They generate the majority of business opportunities and create numerous jobs worldwide. The Asian Development Bank (ADB) reported that, during 2010–2019, MSMEs in Southeast Asia accounted for an average 97% of all enterprises, 69% of the total workforce, and 41% of a country's gross domestic product (GDP). This suggests that the region's robust growth over the past decade was largely underpinned by MSMEs (ADB, 2020a). Thus, MSME development appears to be central to accelerating inclusive growth; and contributing to alleviating poverty across developing Asia. What should governments and international organizations do to stimulate MSME development? What are the impediments to MSME growth in developing countries? The list includes the lack of access to finance, human and managerial capital, and institutional barriers such as market entry and corruption. Due to their small size, MSMEs are inherently constrained in their ability to access credit compared with larger firms. They do not have as large collaterals to borrow money as large firms can afford. The lack of reliable credit information or weak legal institutions also limit financing options. Bruhn et al. (2010) points to the lack of managerial capital as an impediment to firm growth and stresses the role management resources play in improving the choice and productivity of other production inputs. On the other hand, Beck et al. (2005) uses firm level survey data from 54 countries to show that weak legal institutions and corruption stifle firm growth, with small firms particularly vulnerable.

Among other constraints, we focus here on the role financing plays in determining firm growth. Due to their small size and absence of collateral, MSMEs are particularly constrained in their ability to access lines of credit compared with larger firms (Ayyagari, Beck, and Demirgüç-Kunt, 2007). Instead, they rely on internal funding or cash from family and friends to finance their business. A large pool of literature emphasizes the importance access to finance has on firm investments and growth as well as overall economic development. Levine (1999), Demirgüç-Kunt and Maksimovic (1998), and Rajan and Zingales (1996) document the relationship at the aggregate level between financial development and economic growth, while Banerjee et al. (2015) and Karlan and Zinman (2010) estimate the impact of access to finance for capital-constrained firms at the micro level. However, empirical evidence is mixed and it is not entirely clear how governments or international organizations can intervene to facilitate MSME financial arrangements. One way to improve the efficiency of loan arrangements and use is through business training programs designed to improve MSME business skills (Prediger and Gut, 2014). However, the causal effect of these programs on business growth and expansion is not necessarily well documented (Mckenzie, 2020). Cho and Honorati (2014) provides evidence that, although these programs improve business knowledge and practices, it is not linked to eventual business growth. Karlan and Valdivia (2011) presents evidence from Peru where a female entrepreneur program led to a salient increase in "bad months" and decline in "good months." Drexler et al. (2014) found simple training (such as imparting "rules of thumb") is effective in increasing business profits, while complex training does not. Shapiro (2019) also shows that business development programs have limited impact on entrepreneurial profits due to a narrow focus on business promoting strategies.

To ensure the optimal provision of credit to MSMEs, one must understand why credit markets allow MSMEs to suffer from an inability to access funds or face usury interest rates. There are three main issues that stem from information asymmetry in credit markets: (i) adverse selection, (ii) moral hazard, and (iii) imperfect contract enforcement (Hoff and Stiglitz, 1990). Due to inherent asymmetric information between borrowers and lenders, lenders cannot easily distinguish safe borrowers from risky ones. This leads to a uniform interest rate structure where safe borrowers can expect a net loss and leave the market, thereby leaving only risky borrowers in the credit market. This is the adverse selection problem. In contrast, moral hazard refers to the situation where lenders cannot monitor a borrower's effort level or whether loans are used properly. Borrowers may not strictly adhere to their repayment responsibilities and engage in risky activities where costs are born by lenders. Imperfect contract enforcement, in the context of lending and borrowing, means that lenders have difficulty in strictly enforcing repayments, even in the absence of adverse selection and moral hazard problems. Borrowers have an incentive to default on loans if the penalty is small.

In the 1980s and 1990s, microcredit programs attracted wide attention because of their ability to overcome these barriers. They had surprisingly high repayment rates even without collateral. One theoretically proven mechanism is peer selection, mutual peer monitoring, and a social sanction mechanism of joint liability arrangement. This helped prevent adverse selection, moral hazard, and strategic default (Armendáriz de Aghion and Morduch, 2010). A typical lending group would consist of several borrowers with a joint liability structure. A lender can choose his or her own group of diligent and trustworthy fellow members. In the course of repayment, they monitor each other. This system exploits the feature that information asymmetry is less salient between borrowers than between a borrower and a lender. In addition, failure to complete repayment usually leads to social ostracism and hence prevents strategic default.[1] Despite high repayment rates, it is difficult to identify the causal impact of microcredit on poverty reduction, in general. Empirical evidence is mixed (Banerjee, Karlan, and Zinman, 2015), and at some point the program's inflexible repayment schedule and stringent requirement conditions inhibit investment in high-return, illiquid business opportunities among the poor (Field et al. 2013). Karlan and Zinman (2009) documented the presence of moral hazard in a large-scale randomized controlled trial conducted in South Africa. Furthermore, Giné and Karlan (2014) found no clear difference between group and individual lending, evidence contradictory to the theoretical foundation of peer screening, monitoring, and enforcement.

The novel financial technology (fintech)-based loan covered in this report is another attempt to overcome these barriers and enhance the flow of capital to those with profitable business opportunities. The report analyzes the case of self-employed tricycle drivers in the Philippines. The main objectives of the study are to (i) assess how fintech can improve living standards and the social welfare of tricycle drivers—and support the development of regional economies in the Philippines, and (ii) explore a possible financing model for the self-employed based on the findings of a baseline survey of tricycle drivers. The survey was conducted on drivers with and without access to fintech loans during November–December 2019. The report analyzes the effect of the loan program on the well-being of drivers who opted to take out loans. The remainder of the report is organized as follows: Section 2 provides a basic description of the fintech loan program; Sections 3 and 4 examine related literature and reviews the methodology used in the study; Section 5 presents the profile of surveyed drivers and compares drivers who applied for the fintech program with those who did not; Section 6 uses multiple regressions to analyze the impact of fintech loans on driver welfare and regional economic development; and Section 7 examines financing models for the self-employed, followed by a concluding section.

---

[1]   For detailed literature on each mechanism, for peer screening, see Armendariz de Aghion and Gollier, 2000; Gangopadhyay et al. 2005; Ghatak, 1999; Guttman, 2008; Van Tassel, 1999; for peer monitoring, see Stiglitz, 1990; Banerjee et al. 1994; and for peer enforcement, see Armendariz de Aghion, 1999; Besley and Coate, 1995.

2. Fintech Loans

The fintech loan scheme covered in this report aims to overcome three barriers associated with information asymmetry. Instead of relying on social structure, such as joint liability, the new loan program adopts a recent breakthrough in Internet of Things (IoT) technology to alleviate moral hazard and imperfect payment enforcement. The key innovation that sets it apart from conventional auto-loans is that drivers can access collateral-free auto-financing because of a remote control IoT device able to safely deactivate a motorcycle engine should a driver fail to repay. With the device connected to a Mobility Cloud Connecting System, the lender or the fintech firm can remotely access certain tricycle information—such as global positioning system (GPS) coordinates, the distance traveled, time in operation, battery, speed, and engine oil condition. It allows constant monitoring of borrowers and thus significantly reduces monitoring costs. The information gives lenders the ability to overcome informational disadvantages over work behavior, thus helping overcome moral hazard. Additionally, if there is a failure in meeting payment obligations, the motorcycle can be deactivated and confiscated once safely parked. The knowledge that drivers cannot simply escape their payment responsibilities while keeping the tricycle motivates them to work hard to meet the payment schedule. It also allows the fintech firm to safely recoup most of the loan amount should drivers abandon the loan program. This enables better contract enforcement.

The new fintech loan program is currently marketed by Japanese fintech solution provider Global Mobility Service (GMS). The firm is reaching out to tricycle drivers with little access to financing or loans from formal financial institutions, such as commercial banks. It broadly targets those with no other access to financing but may have the means to repay. This offers a financing avenue to poor people who can work as a tricycle driver, but do not have the means to finance the vehicle. It can also be a stepping stone for poor people to build a credit history and progress in a career. This report estimates the impact the new financing scheme has on driver well-being and, more generally, regional economic development.

3. Literature Review

"Fintech" refers to an industry where companies use recent technological development to increase financial system efficiency and increase access to new financial products. Although the concept of using technology to widen financial opportunities is not new—with examples like credit cards or automated teller machines—fintech has gained wide attention in recent years. With an explosion of firms worldwide combining traditional financial products with technological advances, such as new generations of mobile phone networks and online platforms for financial settlement, they are better equipped to provide new financial products to more customers more efficiently. For development and poverty reduction, this opens a new window of opportunity. Mobile money service providers can now offer a semi-bank account to the previously unbanked, enabling them to safely store money and transfer funds at affordable rates. Entrepreneurs and small businesses gain access to a variety of credit sources through crowdfunding and alternative credit scoring systems that promote regional development. Though examples abound, fintech remains relatively new, and more rigorous academic evidence of poverty reduction is needed. This section reviews a growing body of literature that investigates how financial technologies enable more efficient delivery of financial services to more customers—and their impact on regional development and poverty reduction.

The most prominent example of widely used fintech in poor people's daily life is mobile money. Mobile money is a financial service usually operated on mobile devices that enables saving, transferring, and paying money quickly and safely. One example is a mobile phone-based transfer service, called M-PESA, commonly used in Kenya and Tanzania. Focusing on the application's money-transferring capability, a series of papers examine its impact on the welfare of mobile money users. For example, Suri et al. (2012) shows how the fast adoption of M-PESA in Kenya helps users respond better to adverse health shocks. It finds that users can tap into remittances to finance health payments without sacrificing other important expenditures, such as food and education. The risk-sharing effect of easier and more affordable remittance payments is also shown by Jack and Suri (2014). Mobile money users show larger amounts of remittances from more diverse sources given a negative income shock. While non-users experience a decrease in consumption, remittances between families and friends dispersed over large distances acts as insurance—mobile money users do not reduce their consumption.

The informal insurance or risk-sharing effect of remitting mobile money is also shown in Tanzania among villages facing a local rainfall shock. Family and social networks scattered across different villages help cope with village-level shocks using money transfers, but the spillover within villages between users and non-users was not observed (Riley 2018). A more dramatic example of risk sharing is shown in Blumenstock et al. (2016), which witnessed the immediate transfer of prepaid cellular phone minutes to people influenced by an earthquake in Rwanda. Munyegera and Matsumoto (2015) find that mobile money has a positive effect on real per capita consumption through increased frequency and remittance amounts in Uganda.

Given mobile money's safe storing and payment functions, positive effects other than risk sharing must be present. While up-to-date evidence concentrates on transfer capability, Suri (2017) mentions other potential effects, such as larger savings as money can be safely stored and the better allocation of human capital through lower migration costs. Using a quantitative dynamic general equilibrium model using Kenyan firm-level data, Beck et al. (2018) explains its potential to boost entrepreneurial growth and macroeconomic development. Gosavi (2018) notes the adoption of mobile money service by small firms in eastern sub-Saharan Africa, and finds those using the service are more likely to obtain loans or lines of credit.

Unlike mobile money services, the fintech used in our Philippine setting is more related to credit markets with existing lending industries. As mentioned, the credit market suffers mainly from adverse selection, moral hazard, and enforcement of payment. To our knowledge, while there does not appear to be an academic paper specifically addressing the causal impact of this fintech on regional development, we show how fintech improved the accessibility of households and firms to the credit market. Since the use of fintech in microloan programs has been still thin in developing countries as opposed to mobile money, we believe our study makes a good contribution to the literature.

One way is the use of a credit scoring system that deals with adverse selection in credit markets. While the practice of assigning scores to households and firms for creditworthiness is common (Frame et al. 2001), recent technologies and the widespread use of computers and mobile phones make it possible to use factors other than traditional variables related to financial status to assess the ability to repay loans. One example is the digital footprint. Berg et al. (2018) examine the predictive power of simple and easily accessible digital footprints, such as the type of operating system used, mistakes in typing email addresses, and whether one clicks on website advertisements (for example, shopping). Despite the high cost-effectiveness in gathering these data compared to traditional factors, these digital variables are highly predictive of loan repayment abilities—and they contain information complementary to traditional variables used to measure credit bureau scores. In addition, the discriminatory power of digital footprint-based scores are similar between unscorable and scorable customers. This has important implications for financial inclusion and reducing inequality. The potential to assess the creditworthiness of people without a conventional credit history can improve accessibility to credit markets. Another study conducted by Agarwal et al. (2019) also investigates the effectiveness of mobile footprints and finds predictive power that outperforms traditional credit scores in assessing loan approvals and possible defaults.

4. Methodology

The data used in this report come from survey on tricycle drivers across the National Capital Region (NCR), otherwise known as Metropolitan Manila. A set of questionnaires was developed to measure the tricycle drivers' demographic and socioeconomic characteristics. The survey was conducted November–December 2019 and was administered by Orient Integrated Development Consultants, Inc. (OIDCI), a consulting firm in Quezon City, which followed the close instructions of the ADB research team.

The survey sample mainly consists of two groups. One is a group of randomly sampled drivers from the City of Manila (Manila) and Quezon City. All drivers belong to a tricycle operators and drivers' association (TODA) that consented to participate in the survey. Approximately 8 to 10 drivers per TODA were randomly sampled for interviews. They became the main subjects of survey and analysis. The second group is composed of tricycle drivers availing of fintech loans from GMS. They applied for fintech loans to purchase tricycles and are in the repayment process. For the sake of brevity, the first group of drivers will be called conventional drivers and the second group fintech drivers. Conventional drivers are exclusively from Manila and Quezon City, while fintech drivers are widely spread across the NCR's different cities (Table 1).

The survey contents include various characteristics of the tricycle drivers. Basic demographic information is collected through a set of standard questions on the drivers and their household members. Their socioeconomic status is also measured through various questions on different sources of income, household assets, and working behavior. For those who took out loans to finance the tricycle purchase, repayment activities were examined as well. We also measure basic cognitive skills, numeracy, and financial literacy through a set of standard questions. Cognitive skills are tested by four questions from the test of Raven's Progressive Matrices. Numeracy is measured by eight questions on rudimentary arithmetic calculations. Financial literacy is measured by standard questions from the OECD/INFE Toolkit for measuring financial literacy and financial inclusion. One focus is the impact the new financing method had on a drivers' financial inclusion. Of particular interest is whether access to new types of loans could encourage drivers to save more and save using an account at a formal financial institution. For the sake of measuring these potential impacts, the questionnaire contained questions on multifaceted financial inclusion.

Lastly, fundamental economic measures of preference, such as risk preference, time preference, and economic rationality are measured. The motivation is to measure the fundamental preferences that shape decisions to save, borrow, and consume. For this, a great deal of economic experiments usually carried out in lab settings were conducted in the field under the supervision of the ADB research team. Following Choi et al. (2007), 20 questions on budget allocations between two assets with risk were used to elicit risk preference and to test the drivers' basic understanding of risk. Additionally, 30 questions on budget allocation between two distinct time frames were used to measure time preference. Fifteen questions were asked to choose between the specific day and 50 days later, and 15 questions were asked to choose between 50 days later and 100 days later, with the same payment options. The motivation is to capture the potential time-inconsistent preferences, such as present bias or future bias and their impact on financing choices. Another advantage of using a graphic budget allocation tool for eliciting preferences is that it lends itself to an analysis of economic rationality. For each driver, we can compute the Critical

Cost Efficiency Index (CCEI) developed by Afriat (1972), which summarizes the extent to which choices made by drivers violate the Generalized Axiom of Revealed Preference (GARP). It can be used as a proxy of the level of economic rationality of tricycle drivers.

Estimating the impact of fintech loans on driver welfare is carried out in two steps. First, in the profile of surveyed drivers, comparisons are made between fintech and conventional drivers along various dimensions. The difference in sample means will be discussed to examine the size and statistical significance of the difference. Next, in the analysis of a fintech loan's impact, multiple regressions with different models will be used to estimate the fintech loan's contribution to improving driver welfare. This allows the estimation of how much the fintech loan leads to an increase in daily net salary, financial inclusion, and savings.

Table 1: Geographic Distribution of Drivers and TODAs within the National Capital Region

City/Municipality	Drivers		TODAs	
	Conventional	Fintech	Conventional	Fintech
Caloocan		19		6
Makati		18		5
Malabon		1		1
Mandaluyong		3		2
Manila	1,360	199	148	42
Navotas		6		6
Pasay		29		13
Pasig		3		2
Pateros		7		3
Quezon	829	13	85	8
Total	2,189	298	233	88

TODA = tricycle operators and drivers' association.

Note: The table shows the number of drivers and the number of TODAs included in the survey by different cities in Metropolitan Manila.

Source: Asian Development Bank.

5. Profile of Surveyed Drivers

This section gives a summary profile of the sample of drivers and separate descriptive statistics for fintech and conventional driver groups. The purpose is to provide an overall picture of the sampled drivers and to compare drivers who availed of fintech loan from GMS with drivers who did not. One should note that the difference between the two types of drivers may not imply the causal effect of a fintech loan. Rather, it is a combination of the effect of fintech loan and the selection of certain types of drivers in applying for the fintech loan. The comparisons will be made with respect to basic demographic information and socioeconomic variables. The results of experiments conducted alongside the interview will also be discussed.

(i)   Demographic Information

As mentioned, our sample of 2,487 drivers consists of two main groups, conventional drivers from either Manila or Quezon City, and fintech drivers dispersed across different cities in the NCR (Table 2). Their age ranges from 18–79 years old with a mean age of 43 years old. Most are male—there were just 36 female drivers in the sample. The majority of drivers are married with an average 4.5 members in their household (including the driver). The survey defines "household" as a group of people living together for more than 3 months during the past 12 months and share the same source of food. About half have always lived in the NCR, while the remaining half came from different provinces. More than 80% of drivers surveyed reported they were in good or very good physical health.

Their mean education level is 9.6 years, with 60% completing at least 10 years of education—the highest education level before entering university under the Philippine education system.[2] Compared with regular schooling, technical and vocational education was less common. About 20% of drivers received some form of vocational education with the most common type in electronics, followed by automotive training.

There were differences between fintech and conventional drivers. Fintech drivers with access to loans through GMS were slightly younger. In terms of family background, they were more likely to be married and have more household members. They were also more likely to have moved to the NCR from a different province, probably in search of work.

(ii)   Household Assets

We examine the ownership of particular household assets indicative of economic status. They also hinted at possible mechanisms through which they engage in tricycle driving and other financial activities—as assets are usually required for collateral for borrowing in developing countries. The overwhelming majority of drivers (90%) possess a cellular phone. This was higher than owning a refrigerator (42%), a near necessity in the Philippines.

---

[2]   This was the system before it changed to K-12 program in 2013 where one needs 12 years of education before entering college.

There are several types of mobile accounts in the Philippines—such as GCash and PayMaya—that can be used as a semi-bank account for savings and daily transaction payments. However, this service is only available with a smartphone. Thus, among cellular phone owners, 70% used smartphones, while the other 30% owned a phone that does not support internet connections. Lastly, about 43% of drivers owned their home.

A comparison between fintech and conventional drivers suggests that fintech drivers are slightly more likely to have a phone. However, the ownership rate of smartphones barely differs. Fintech drivers are also more likely to own their house, but are less likely to own a refrigerator.

Table 2: Demographic Information and Household Assets

Item	Total	Fintech (1)	Conventional (2)	Difference (1) - (2)
Demographic variables				
Age	42.83	40.26	43.18	-2.91**
	(11.42)	(11.01)	(11.43)	(0.68)
Male	0.99	0.98	0.99	-0.01
	(0.12)	(0.14)	(0.12)	(0.01)
Married	0.83	0.93	0.81	0.11**
	(0.38)	(0.26)	(0.39)	(0.02)
Number of household members	4.45	4.89	4.39	0.5**
	(2.11)	(2.17)	(2.10)	(0.13)
Living in the birth province	0.55	0.35	0.57	-0.22**
	(0.50)	(0.48)	(0.49)	(0.03)
Physical health good	0.82	0.86	0.81	0.05*
	(0.39)	(0.35)	(0.39)	(0.02)
Years of education	9.60	8.74	9.72	-0.98**
	(3.02)	(3.30)	(2.96)	(0.20)
Technical and vocational education	0.20	0.19	0.20	-0.02
	(0.40)	(0.39)	(0.40)	(0.02)
Household assets				
Refrigerator	0.42	0.33	0.43	-0.1**
	(0.49)	(0.47)	(0.50)	(0.03)
Cell phone	0.97	0.99	0.96	0.03**
	(0.18)	(0.10)	(0.19)	(0.01)
Smartphone	0.61	0.62	0.61	0.01
	(0.49)	(0.49)	(0.49)	(0.03)
House	0.43	0.53	0.41	0.12**
	(0.49)	(0.50)	(0.49)	(0.03)
Observations	2,487	298	2,189	

Note: The table shows the mean of demographic and household asset variables for the entire driver sample, conventional drivers, and fintech drivers. 'Physical health good' is a dummy for reporting 'good' or 'very good' health. Technical and vocational education is also a dummy for receiving one. Household asset variables are all dummies indicating ownership of the identified assets. Standard deviations are shown in parentheses below the mean. The last column shows the mean difference between the two groups ("Fintech" minus "Conventional"), and the standard error of difference is reported in parentheses. ** and* represent 5% and 1% significance, respectively.

Source: Asian Development Bank.

(iii) Financial Attitude

The questionnaire includes extensive questions on personality traits, attitudes, and subjective expectations to help assess financial attitude. Field interviewers read aloud a series of statements that describe certain financial behaviors with drivers responding whether they strongly agree, agree, neither agree nor disagree, disagree, or strongly disagree (Figure 1).

There were three statements that described impulsive spending and a profligate lifestyle. To these questions, drivers on average answered 'neither agree nor disagree.'[3] However, there were other four contrary statements describing careful planning for the future and a frugal lifestyle, with drivers on average answering 'agree.'[4] On the question of willingness to take risks, drivers on average agreed they are prepared to take monetary risks to make investments.[5]

As shown in Table 3, the comparison between fintech and conventional drivers show a negligible difference in response to impulsive habits. However, on being economical and in risk taking, significantly more fintech drivers identify themselves as having economical habits and are willing to take risks.

Figure 1: Scale for Attitude Questions

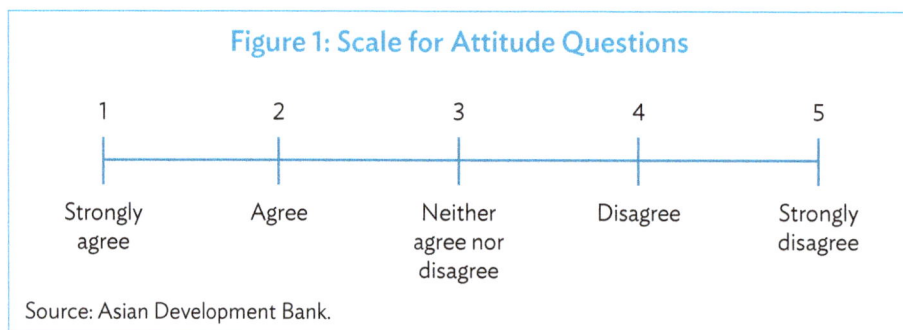

1	2	3	4	5
Strongly agree	Agree	Neither agree nor disagree	Disagree	Strongly disagree

Source: Asian Development Bank.

Table 3: Financial Attitudes

Item	Total	Fintech (1)	Conventional (2)	Difference (1) - (2)
Impulsive habit	2.94	2.88	2.95	-0.07
	(0.86)	(0.85)	(0.86)	(0.05)
Economic habit	1.74	1.66	1.75	-0.09**
	(0.49)	(0.48)	(0.49)	(0.03)
Risk taking	2.09	1.94	2.11	-0.17**
	(0.99)	(0.94)	(1.00)	(0.06)
Observations	2,487	298	2,189	

Note: The table shows the mean scores among financial attitude questions for the entire sample of drivers, conventional drivers, and fintech drivers. Standard deviations are shown in parentheses below the mean. The last column shows the mean difference between the two groups ("Fintech" minus "Conventional"), and the standard error of difference is reported in parentheses. ** and* represent 5% and 1% significance, respectively.

Source: Asian Development Bank.

---

[3]   An example statement reads "I tend to live for today and let tomorrow take care of itself."
[4]   An example statement reads "Before I buy something, I carefully consider whether I can afford it."
[5]   The statement reads "I am prepared to risk some of my own money when saving or making an investment."

(iv) Household Decision-Making

The questionnaire includes a series of questions on joint decision-making between drivers and their spouse/partner. We specifically ask the relative decision-making power between them in the purchase of several categories of goods and services. A ruler shaped figure was used to assist in understanding a driver's answer (Figure 2). We also considered the case in which the good or service was not purchased in the past 12 months. The result (Table 4) is for male fintech and male conventional drivers. Zero corresponds to the decision made by the wife/female partner alone and 10 the decision made by husband/male partner alone.

Figure 2: Ruler Figure for Measuring Household Decision-Making Power

Note: The figure shows the ruler image used to ask drivers about joint decision-making between the husband/male partner or wife/female partner.

Source: Asian Development Bank.

Table 4: Household Decision-Making Power

Item	Total	Fintech (1)	Conventional (2)	Difference (1) - (2)
Overall decisions about money	5.07	5.04	5.07	-0.03
	(3.09)	(3.17)	(3.08)	(0.21)
Food and non-alcoholic beverage	4.29	4.18	4.31	-0.14
	(3.21)	(3.33)	(3.19)	(0.22)
Alcoholic beverage and tobacco	8.12	7.97	8.14	-0.17
	(2.45)	(2.52)	(2.44)	(0.21)
Clothing and footwear	3.38	3.29	3.39	-0.10
	(2.77)	(2.76)	(2.77)	(0.19)
Furnishings and goods for household maintenance	2.43	2.45	2.42	0.03
	(2.41)	(2.34)	(2.42)	(0.16)
Health products (e.g., medicine, hospital visit)	3.92	4.05	3.90	0.15
	(2.97)	(3.14)	(2.94)	(0.21)
Children's education	5.06	5.01	5.07	-0.06
	(2.98)	(3.17)	(2.95)	(0.24)
Furniture and equipment	5.01	5.24	4.98	0.26
	(2.92)	(2.95)	(2.92)	(0.21)
Observation	1,666	234	1,432	

Note: The table reports average scores reported by male drivers from the total sample, conventional drivers, and fintech drivers. The score summarizes the relative decision-making power between husband/male partner and wife/female partner in purchasing decisions of different categories of commodities and services. Standard deviations are shown in parentheses below the mean. The last column shows the mean difference between the two groups ("Fintech" minus "Conventional"), and the standard error of difference is reported in parentheses. ** and* represent 5% and 1% significance, respectively.

Source: Asian Development Bank.

The average score is reported for only male drivers. It generally shows that wives/female partners have more decision-making power across all categories except alcoholic beverage and tobacco. Although subjects respond that they have equal power overall in decisions about money, they admit that wives/female partners in general have more decision-making power for specific categories (except alcoholic beverages and tobacco). Although the self-reported measure, especially from the husband/male partner side alone, does not reveal the true decision-making dynamics within households, it shows the general tendency of decision-making perceived by the husband/male partner. For the sake of comparison, we also report the average scores reported by fintech drivers and conventional drivers separately. There is no significant difference in any of the categories.

(v) Cognitive Skills, Numeracy, and Financial Literacy

There were three sections designed to test drivers' cognitive skills, numeracy, and financial literacy. Cognitive skills were tested by four questions from Raven's Progressive Matrices, a non-verbal group test to measure abstract reasoning and fluid intelligence. The numeracy test is aimed at measuring elementary skills in dealing with numbers. The section contained eight questions ranging from basic one digit addition to complicated addition and multiplication. Financial literacy was tested based on 10 questions from the OECD/INFE International Survey of Adult Financial Literacy Competencies. The average scores among all drivers were 1.6 questions out of 4 in the Raven's test, 4.7 questions out of 8 in the numeracy test and 4.8 questions out of 10 in the financial literacy test (Table 5).

The comparison between fintech and conventional drivers show that fintech drivers generally have slightly lower levels of cognitive and numeracy skills. Out of 4 Raven's test questions, conventional drivers scored 1.6 questions, while fintech drivers scored 1.4 questions. For numeracy questions, of 8 questions, conventional drivers scored 4.7 questions on average, while fintech drivers scored 4.4 questions. Hence, fintech drivers scored, on average, 0.2 and 0.3 questions less than conventional drivers in the Raven's and numeracy test sections, respectively, with the differences statistically significant at the 1% level. As for financial literacy, fintech drivers once again scored slightly lower than conventional drivers, but the difference was statistically negligible.

Table 5: Test Scores and Experimental Measures

Item	Total	Fintech (1)	Conventional (2)	Difference (1) – (2)
Test section score				
Raven's test	1.59	1.41	1.61	−0.20**
	(1.29)	(1.24)	(1.30)	(0.08)
Numeracy test	4.70	4.43	4.74	−0.31**
	(1.89)	(1.88)	(1.89)	(0.12)
Financial literacy test	4.81	4.76	4.82	−0.07
	(1.34)	(1.44)	(1.32)	(0.09)
Experimental measure				
Risk preference	0.588	0.594	0.587	0.008
	(0.085)	(0.086)	(0.085)	(0.005)
Impatience	0.382	0.388	0.381	0.007
	(0.197)	(0.188)	(0.199)	(0.012)

continued on next page

Table 5 continued

Item	Total	Fintech (1)	Conventional (2)	Difference (1) - (2)
CCEI from risk preference section	0.847	0.831	0.850	-0.019
	(0.192)	(0.200)	(0.191)	(0.012)
CCEI from time preference section	0.854	0.841	0.856	-0.015
	(0.149)	(0.151)	(0.149)	(0.009)
Observation	2,487	298	2,189	

CCEI = Critical Cost Efficiency Index.

Note: The table shows the three test scores and four experimental measures among the entire driver sample, conventional drivers, and fintech drivers. Standard deviations are shown in parentheses below the mean. The last column shows the mean difference between the two groups ("Fintech" minus "Conventional"), and the standard error of difference is reported in parentheses. ** and* represent 5% and 1% significance, respectively.

Source: Asian Development Bank.

(vi) Risk Preference, Time Preference, and Economic Rationality

Finally, we examine the experimental result from two experiments: risk preference and time preference. The main novelty of the baseline survey is the adoption of lab experiments in the field to measure risk and time preferences. Experiments on risk preference contain 20 questions and experiments on time preference contain 30 questions. Both sections present a series of graphic budget allocation questions between two states of nature. In the risk preference section, one is asked to allocate a given budget between two risky assets, whereas in the time preference section, one needs to allocate between two periods. Examining the answers reveals both their preference of risk and time, and sheds light on the level of economic rationality.

The risk preference measure used is calculated as an average of the relative share of cheaper goods chosen in each question involving risk. A risk-neutral individual would prefer to choose more of cheaper good despite one-half probability of ending up with a small payoff. The most extreme case would be when all investments are made for cheaper products, in which case the measure would be one. On the other hand, a risk-averse agent would seek to balance the payoff in each situation by purchasing relatively expensive products as well as cheap ones. The most risk-averse agent would always choose an option with an equal payoff in each state, thereby completely hedging the risk. This is a situation with the risk measure one-half. If the risk measure is below half, it implies a choice of options that are stochastically dominated by other options in a question, and hence suggests that a subject is making an irrational choice.

Figure 3 shows the distribution of risk preference for fintech and conventional drivers separately with 0.5 marked by a red vertical line. Of the entire sample, the mean of the distribution is 0.588 and a standard deviation of 0.085. Twelve percent of respondents showed a measure below 0.5. Comparing the risk preference between fintech and conventional drivers, the kernel density plot does not show significant differences in distribution, but fintech drivers appear to have slightly higher means. Indeed, comparing means reveals that fintech drivers have a slightly higher risk preference. Their average risk preference measure was 0.594, higher than the entire group average, while the one for conventional drivers, 0.587, was slightly lower. The t-test for the equality of means fails to reject the equality of means between the two groups at the 10% level.

As for the time preference measure, we compute the impatience measure of each subject. The measure is calculated as the relative share of "sooner" payment amount averaged over 30 questions on the choice between sooner or later payments. Payment amounts are scheduled in a way that rewards later payment. Hence, an impatient individual would prefer to choose more sooner payments despite larger payment amounts promised in the future—we quantify this as an impatience measure between zero and one. In most extreme cases, choosing all sooner payment options would result in measure one with the other extreme resulting in zero. An equal balance between sooner and later payments in all questions would result in 0.5.

The distribution of impatience measure computed from 30 questions are shown in Figure 4 for fintech and conventional drivers with the red vertical line corresponding to 0.5. The mean of the distribution is 0.381, suggesting drivers' willingness to wait for future payment for greater rewards. However, one can also see some mass near impatience measure one in both distributions. This indicates there are a number of people who choose sooner payments in all the 30 questions and suggests the highest degree of impatience. The comparison of average and distribution of impatience between fintech and conventional drivers shows negligible difference between the two.

Lastly, we examine the economic rationality measure, the Critical Cost Efficiency Index (CCEI), which summarizes the degree to which each budget constraint must be relaxed to remove the respondents' violations of the Generalized Axiom of Revealed Preference (GARP). The measure ranges from zero to one. The closer to one, the closer the data are to satisfying GARP. We can compute the CCEI from the choices made from both the risk preference and the time preference experiment. Here, we present both measures, one based on 20 risk preference questions and the other based on 30 time preference questions.

The distribution of CCEI measures based on risk and time preference questions are displayed in Figure 5 and Figure 6, respectively, for fintech and conventional drivers. The distribution in general indicates the majority of drivers exhibit a high level of rationality, with choices mostly satisfying GARP. Among all drivers, the mean of the measure is 0.847 and 0.854, and the standard deviation is 0.192 and 0.149 for CCEI measure based on risk preference and time preference questions respectively.

The comparison between CCEI distributions obtained from risk and time preference experiment suggests larger variations from the risk preference section. Although there are large mass clustered near CCEI measure one in Figure 5, the distribution has a longer tail, indicating larger heterogeneity. The comparison of CCEI measures between fintech and conventional customers reveals that fintech customers, in general, exhibit lower levels of economic rationality than conventional customers. The differences for both measures show that conventional drivers have higher levels of CCEI measures, though the difference was marginally insignificant at the 10% level.

Figure 3: Risk Preference Measure Distribution for Fintech and Conventional Drivers

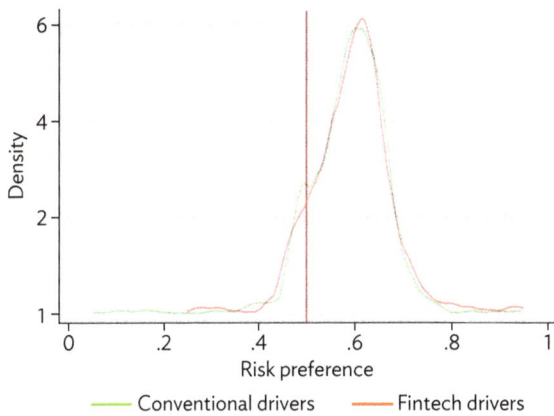

Conventional drivers — Fintech drivers

Note: The figure plots the distribution of risk preference measure for fintech and conventional drivers. Risk-neutral agent would display a risk preference measure of 0.5, and the most risk averse agent would display the measure 1. The red vertical line corresponds to 0.5.

Source: Asian Development Bank.

Figure 4: Impatience Measure Distribution for Fintech and Conventional Drivers

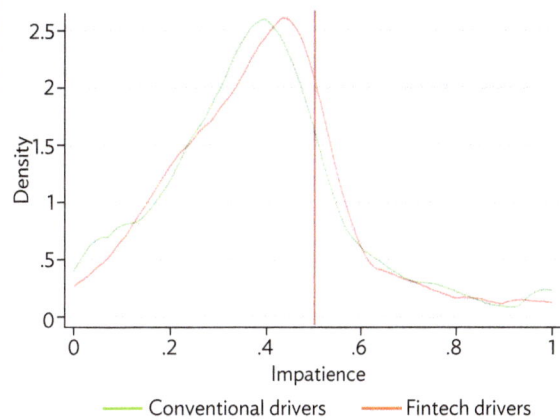

Conventional drivers — Fintech drivers

Note: The figure plots the distribution of impatience measure for fintech and conventional drivers. Choosing early (late) payments in all the questions would result in measure one (zero). The red vertical line corresponds to 0.5 that would be the case if equal amounts are chosen between the two time frames in all questions.

Source: Asian Development Bank.

Figure 5: CCEI Distribution from Risk Preference Section

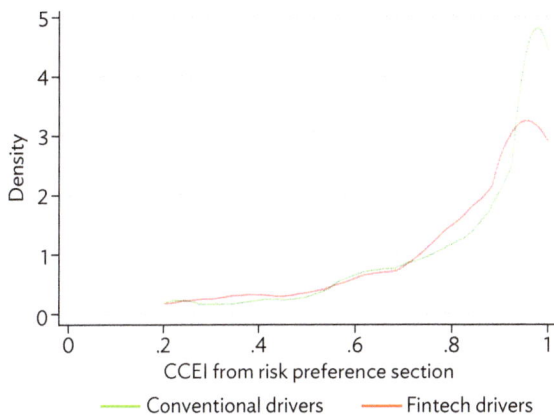

Conventional drivers — Fintech drivers

Note: The figure plots the distribution of the Critical Cost Efficiency Index (CCEI) for fintech and conventional drivers that measures the extent to which choices made by subjects in 20 risk preference experiment questions are close to satisfying the Generalized Axiom of Revealed Preference (GARP).

Source: Asian Development Bank.

Figure 6: CCEI Distribution from Risk Preference Section

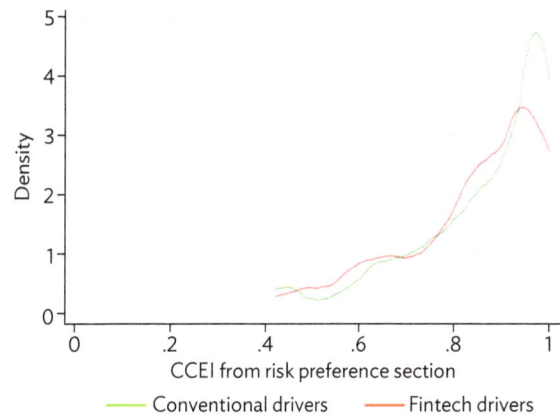

Conventional drivers — Fintech drivers

Note: The figure plots the distribution of the Critical Cost Efficiency Index (CCEI) for fintech and conventional drivers that measures the extent to which choices made by subjects in 30 time preference experiment questions are close to satisfying the Generalized Axiom of Revealed Preference (GARP).

Source: Asian Development Bank.

6. Key Findings from the Baseline Survey

(i)   Impact of Fintech on Drivers' Welfare and Financial Inclusion

This section investigates the impact of fintech loans on a driver's labor market activities, tricycle financing decisions, financial planning, and financial accessibility. The investigation will be carried out in two steps. First, we will simply compare major indicators of the impact of fintech loans on fintech drivers and conventional drivers. This will offer a glimpse of different behaviors between the two types of drivers, but is not an attempt to derive any rigorous causal impact from the fintech loan. The comparison analysis will provide a big picture view of their different driving behaviors and income. It also provides evidence about different financial decision-making as shaped by accessibility to financial products. Second, multivariate linear regression analysis will be used to carefully estimate the causal impact of fintech loans on the outcome variables mentioned. This has the advantage of controlling for all other variables that potentially affect outcome variables. Hence, the estimate produced by the regression analysis allows for a more precise interpretation of the causal effect of fintech loans.

Simple Comparison

First, we review labor market activities—specifically working hours, net salary, and sources of income (Table 6). On average, drivers work 11 hours a day and 6.3 days a week, or 69 working hours per week. There is considerable difference in working hours between fintech and conventional drivers (Figure 7). The difference suggests that fintech drivers work fewer hours than conventional drivers. Fintech drivers work 67.0 hours on average, while conventional drivers work 69.2 hours per week. The 2.2-hour difference was marginally insignificant at the 10% level. Daily variations show that while fintech customers on average may work fewer hours a day, they are likely to work more days a week. We also have data on length of break times during work, which suggest fintech drivers take 15 minutes a day less break than conventional drivers.

The comparison on income between fintech drivers with GMS loans and those who did not is straightforward. Fintech drivers show much higher income from all different sources compared with conventional drivers. The average daily net salary is P572.[6] Fintech customers report an average of P731 of daily net salary compared to P551 for conventional customers. This translates into a P180 difference in favor of fintech drivers, with the difference statistically and economically significant.

Besides their tricycle job, there must be other sources of income for both the driver and household. We asked about monthly aggregate income to compare the monthly income of the driver, spouse, and total household income. First, drivers, who are mostly male, earn much larger sums than their spouse.[7] Restricting the sample to those with spouses, the monthly spouse income is P4,855, still much smaller than the driver's income. Another clear pattern

---

[6]   The dollar–peso exchange rate was roughly $50 = P50 throughout the time of the survey and analysis.
[7]   Those who do not have a spouse are recorded to have zero spousal income.

is that the sum of a driver's and spouse income is less than the total household income. This implies the existence of other sources of household income.

It is clear that fintech drivers have larger incomes. Fintech drivers report, on average, P21,545 of monthly income, P6,360 more than conventional drivers. This is larger than the difference in daily net salaries from the tricycle job corrected to monthly values, which indicates they receive more income from second jobs or other sources. It is interesting that the monthly income of fintech driver spouses is also P3,824 more than spouses of conventional drivers. The difference is both economically and statistically significant. The resulting total household income also indicates that fintech drivers on average earn P11,386 more per month than conventional customers.

Table 6: Labor Market Activities and Income

Item	Total	Fintech (1)	Conventional (2)	Difference (1) - (2)
Working hours/day	10.98	10.44	11.05	-0.60*
	(3.05)	(3.11)	(3.04)	(0.19)
Working days/week	6.25	6.36	6.23	0.13
	(0.92)	(0.92)	(0.92)	(0.06)
Working hours/week	68.98	67.04	69.24	-2.20
	(22.34)	(22.58)	(22.30)	(1.39)
Break time	105.80	92.80	107.58	-14.78**
	(89.38)	(81.17)	(90.32)	(5.08)
Net salary/day	572.26	730.69	550.70	179.99**
	(228.40)	(289.33)	(209.82)	(17.33)
Driver income/month	15,947	21,545	15,185	6,360**
	(8293)	(11415)	(7457)	(679)
Spouse income/month	3,731	7,097	3,273	3,824**
	(8346)	(12852)	(7415)	(760)
Household income/month	26,409	36,431	25,045	11,386**
	(23063)	(47304)	(16883)	(2760)
Observations	2,487	298	2,189	

Note: The table shows the working hours, break time, net salary, and monthly income for the entire sample of drivers, conventional drivers, and fintech drivers. Standard deviations are shown in parentheses below the mean. The last column shows the mean difference between the two groups ("Fintech" minus "Conventional"), and the standard error of difference is reported in parentheses. ** and * represent 5% and 1% significance, respectively.

Source: Asian Development Bank.

Figure 7: Difference in Working Hours between Fintech and Conventional Drivers

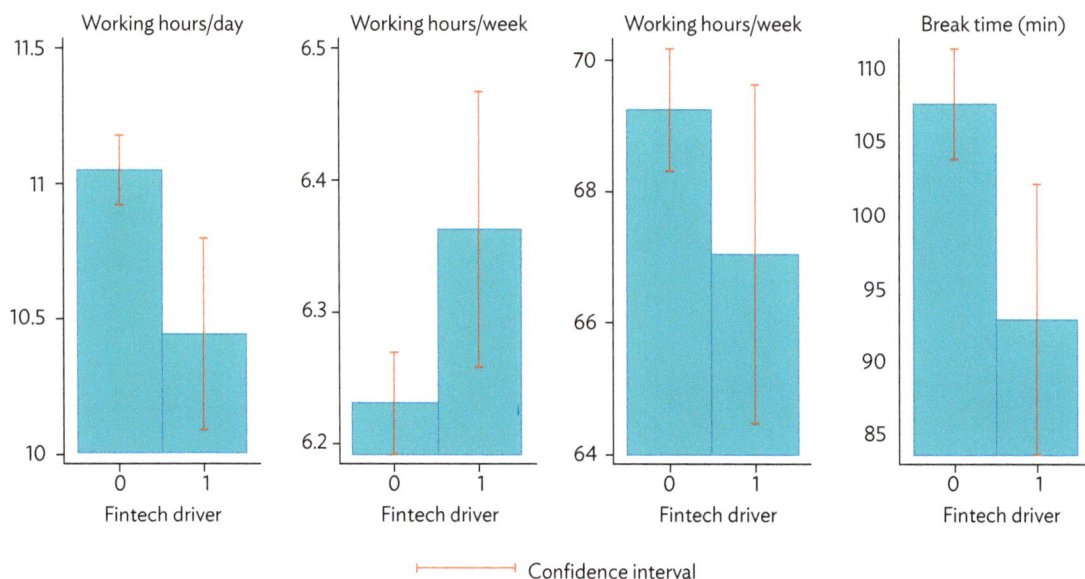

Note: The figure plots the daily working hours, weekly working days and hours, and daily break time in minutes for fintech and conventional drivers. The red vertical lines correspond to 95% confidence interval.

Source: Asian Development Bank.

In addition to working hours and salaries, it is important to get a glimpse of the different aspects of driving behavior and financing methods to understand the comprehensive working behavior and the impact of a fintech loan on a driver's welfare. The questionnaire includes a series of questions on the detailed working environment and the arrangements of tricycles for operation (Table 7). As can be expected, most drivers work a day shift, but a considerable number work both day and night. We performed a t-test on the equality of proportions between the two groups of drivers. The result suggests that there are significantly more night shift drivers among fintech drivers compared with conventional drivers.

Table 7: Distribution of Driver Shifts

Shift	Total	Fintech		Conventional		Difference
	Number	Number	Percent	Number	Percent	
Day	1,730	196	65.8	1,534	70.1	-0.04
Night	152	32	10.7	120	5.5	0.05**
Day and night	605	70	23.5	535	24.4	-0.01
Sum	2,487	298	100.0	2,189	100.0	

Note: The table shows the number and percentage of fintech and conventional drivers working on day shift, night shift, and both day and night shifts. The last column reports the t-test result on the equality of proportion between two types of drivers (the difference is "Fintech" minus "Conventional"). ** and * represent 5% and 1% significance, respectively.

Source: Asian Development Bank.

Asked if they own their tricycle, 72% said they drive their own tricycle. For those that do not possess their own tricycle, they borrow one—called the boundary system. While there are a handful of drivers who borrow rent-free, most pay a daily boundary fee. There were 662 drivers in our sample that operate this way. By definition, none of the fintech drivers use the boundary system as they obtained tricycle ownership through the GMS loan program. The average daily boundary fee is P173. For drivers using their own tricycle for operation, we asked how they financed their tricycle purchase. Figure 8 shows a simple schematic that summarizes the ownership scheme.

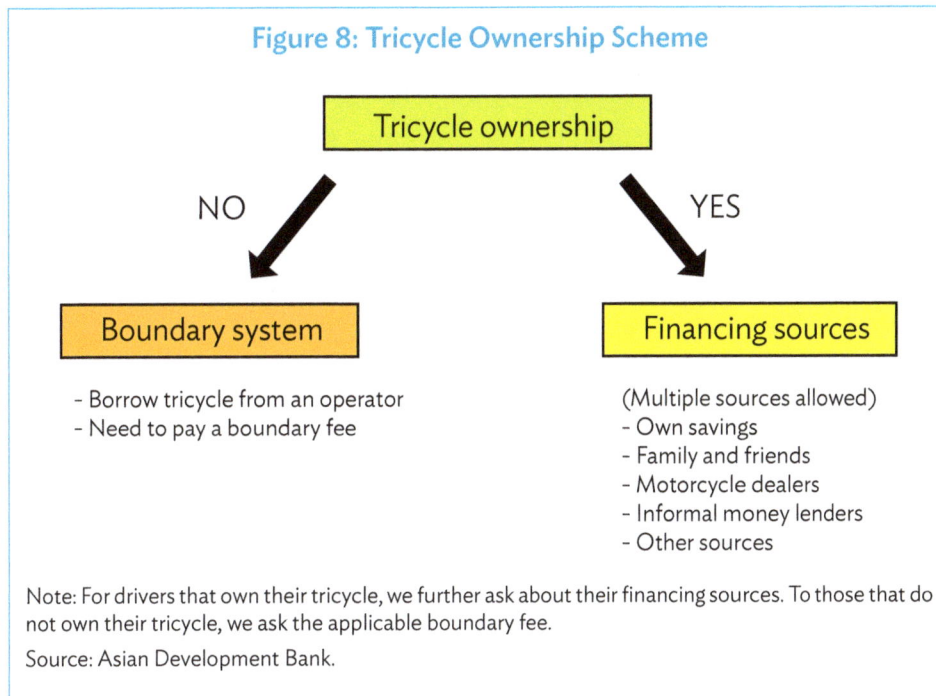

Figure 8: Tricycle Ownership Scheme

Tricycle ownership

NO → Boundary system

- Borrow tricycle from an operator
- Need to pay a boundary fee

YES → Financing sources

(Multiple sources allowed)
- Own savings
- Family and friends
- Motorcycle dealers
- Informal money lenders
- Other sources

Note: For drivers that own their tricycle, we further ask about their financing sources. To those that do not own their tricycle, we ask the applicable boundary fee.
Source: Asian Development Bank.

Table 8 describes the frequency of the financing scheme. Note that there can be multiple financing sources. Hence, the sum of the frequency does not add up to the number of drivers. We also present the percentage of drivers who used each financing source. The last column reports the t-test results on the equality of proportion between the two types of drivers. The result indicates that even for conventional drivers, most financing comes from motorcycle/tricycle dealers. Given the high percentage of own savings and transfers from family and friends, one can infer that the tricycle purchase is commonly financed with a combination of loans from dealers and one's own savings. However, the result for fintech drivers suggests that they resort considerably less on their own savings and transfers from family or their social network. They are more likely to finance the purchase of tricycle entirely with GMS borrowing than conventional drivers, who mix savings, transfers, and borrowing. This difference in financing sources implies a subtle difference in socioeconomic background of the two groups of drivers.

Table 8: Financing Sources

Financing source	Total	Fintech		Conventional		Difference
	Number	Number	Percent	Number	Percent	
Own savings	856	116	38.7	740	49.2	-0.10**
Family members, relatives, and friends	334	17	5.7	317	21.1	-0.15**
Motorcycle/tricycle dealer	953	298	100.0	655	43.5	0.56**
Credit cooperative	7	0	0.0	7	0.5	0.00
Microfinance institution	7	1	0.3	6	0.4	0.00
Pawnshop	0	0	0.0	0	0.0	0.00
Commercial bank	2	0	0.0	2	0.1	0.00
Government loan program	2	0	0.0	2	0.1	0.00
Informal moneylender	54	0	0.0	54	3.6	-0.04**
Gift/donation/inheritance/raffle prize	34	1	0.3	33	2.2	-0.02*

Note: The table shows the number and percentage of fintech and conventional drivers who used the identified financing sources to purchase their tricycle (among drivers that drive their own tricycle for operation). Note that multiple financing sources are allowed. Hence, the sum does not equal to the total number of drivers that drive their own tricycles. The last column reports the t-test result on the equality of proportion between the two types of drivers (the difference is "Fintech" minus "Conventional"). ** and * represent 5% and 1% significance, respectively.

Source: Asian Development Bank.

For those who financed their tricycle by borrowing money from any type of institution or from family and friends, we ask if they are aware of the interest rate. Less than 10% of both fintech and conventional drivers knew their interest rate, and there was no significant difference between the two.

The average loan tenure was 34 months for the entire sample, but there are considerable heterogeneities involved depending on financing source and between fintech and conventional drivers (Table 9). Fintech, on average, had a 45-month repayment period, while conventional drivers had just 29 months. Fintech drivers also have much larger loan amounts. The average estimated loan amount was P277,166 for fintech drivers, and P99,915 for conventional drivers.

Drivers make regular repayments according to payment schedules (Table 10). Monthly and weekly payments are the most common arrangement followed by daily repayments. Note that for conventional drivers, monthly payments are the most common arrangement, whereas for fintech drivers, weekly payments are the dominant arrangement. Depending on repayment frequency, the amount also varies. Large differences in total loan amounts means that fintech drivers make larger regular payments. The data support the observation. Comparisons between weekly payers indicate significantly larger payments made by fintech drivers. Given that most conventional drivers repay monthly rather than weekly, we adjust the weekly payment amounts to monthly levels and compare these amounts between the two types of drivers. The result still indicates that fintech drivers pay significantly larger amounts.

Table 9: Loan Repayment Variables

Item	Total	Fintech (1)	Conventional (2)	Difference (1) - (2)
Loan tenure	33.67	45.06	29.38	15.67**
	(12.33)	(11.85)	(9.44)	(0.77)
Total loan amount	148,464	277,166	99,915	177,250**
	(117356)	(120866)	(69707)	(7423)
Payment amount/week	1,410	1,439	1,225	214*
	(346)	(289)	(559)	(84)
Payment amount/month	4,138	6,114	3,292	2,822**
	(1888)	(1448)	(1344)	(99)
Observation	1,088	298	790	

Note: The table shows loan tenure, the total loan amount, weekly repayment amounts, and monthly payment amounts for the entire sample of drivers, conventional drivers, and fintech drivers. 'Payment amount/week' is averaged among weekly payers. 'Payment amount/month' is averaged among weekly and monthly payers after adjusting the weekly value to monthly values. Standard deviations are shown in parentheses below the mean. The last column shows the mean difference between the two groups ("Fintech" minus "Conventional"), and the standard error of difference is reported in parentheses. ** and * represent 5% and 1% significance, respectively.

Source: Asian Development Bank.

Table 10: Repayment Frequency

Repayment frequency	Fintech Drivers			Conventional Drivers			Difference
	Number	Percent	Payment Amount	Number	Percent	Payment Amount	
Daily	3	1.0	487	95	12.0	188	-0.11**
Weekly	282	94.6	1,439	45	5.7	1,225	0.89**
Bimonthly	0	0.0		3	0.4	3,083	0.00
Monthly	13	4.4	3,081	644	81.4	3,150	-0.77**
Quarterly	0	0.0		3	0.4	8,500	0.00
Sum	298	100.0		790	100.0		

Note: The table shows the number and percentage of repayment frequency with their respective average payment amounts for conventional and fintech drivers. The last column reports the t-test result on the equality of proportions between two types of drivers (the difference is "Fintech" minus "Conventional"). ** and * represent 5% and 1% significance, respectively.

Source: Asian Development Bank.

Next, we review the drivers' financial plans and goals. The questions concern the existence of a budget for financial planning, along with financial goals and actions taken to meet those goals (Table 11). The majority of drivers make some financial plan through budgeting, but few have specific financial goals. When we look at how drivers achieve their financial goals, the most common way is to save money and cut back on spending.

For those with loans and obligations to regularly repay, making financial plans for oneself and the household is helpful for not falling behind on repayments or managing finances. So it is reasonable to expect that those with loans are more likely to be economical and manage their income and expenditures. Here, we test this hypothesis.

First, we compare answers to the question "Does your household have a budget?". Field interviewers also provided a brief explanation about the meaning of the term "budget." Fintech drivers are significantly more likely to have a household budget (Figure 9), with 77% using a budget against 71% of conventional drivers.

Next, we examine whether people have financial goals and are working to reach them. Fintech drivers were more than 12 percentage points higher in having a financial goal compared with conventional drivers. For those with goals, we also asked if they were making any effort to meet them, such as preparing a plan of action, saving money, looking for new jobs, and cutting back on spending. There were negligible differences between the two groups, except to the question of whether one had identified a source of credit. Fintech drivers reported significantly lower positive responses—likely the result of already having a large obligation on their tricycle loan.

Table 11: Financial Planning

Item	Total	Fintech (1)	Conventional (2)	Difference (1) - (2)
Have a budget	0.72	0.77	0.71	0.05*
	(0.45)	(0.42)	(0.45)	(0.03)
Have a financial goal	0.45	0.55	0.43	0.12*
	(0.50)	(0.50)	(0.50)	(0.03)
Prepared a plan of action	0.77	0.77	0.77	0.00
	(0.42)	(0.42)	(0.42)	(0.04)
Increased credit card or loan payment	0.03	0.04	0.03	0.01
	(0.16)	(0.19)	(0.16)	(0.02)
Saved or invested money	0.76	0.74	0.77	-0.03
	(0.42)	(0.44)	(0.42)	(0.04)
Looked for additional work	0.36	0.39	0.35	0.04
	(0.48)	(0.49)	(0.48)	(0.04)
Identified a source of credit	0.09	0.04	0.10	-0.07**
	(0.29)	(0.19)	(0.31)	(0.02)
Cut back on spending	0.79	0.74	0.80	-0.06
	(0.41)	(0.44)	(0.40)	(0.04)
Observation	2,487	298	2,189	

Note: The table shows whether the driver has a budget and financial goal. For those with a financial goal, we ask which action the driver had taken to meet the goal. Standard deviations are shown in parentheses below the mean. The last column shows the mean difference between the two groups ("Fintech" minus "Conventional"), and the standard error of difference is reported in parentheses. ** and * represent 5% and 1% significance, respectively.

Source: Asian Development Bank.

Figure 9: Differences in Financial Planning

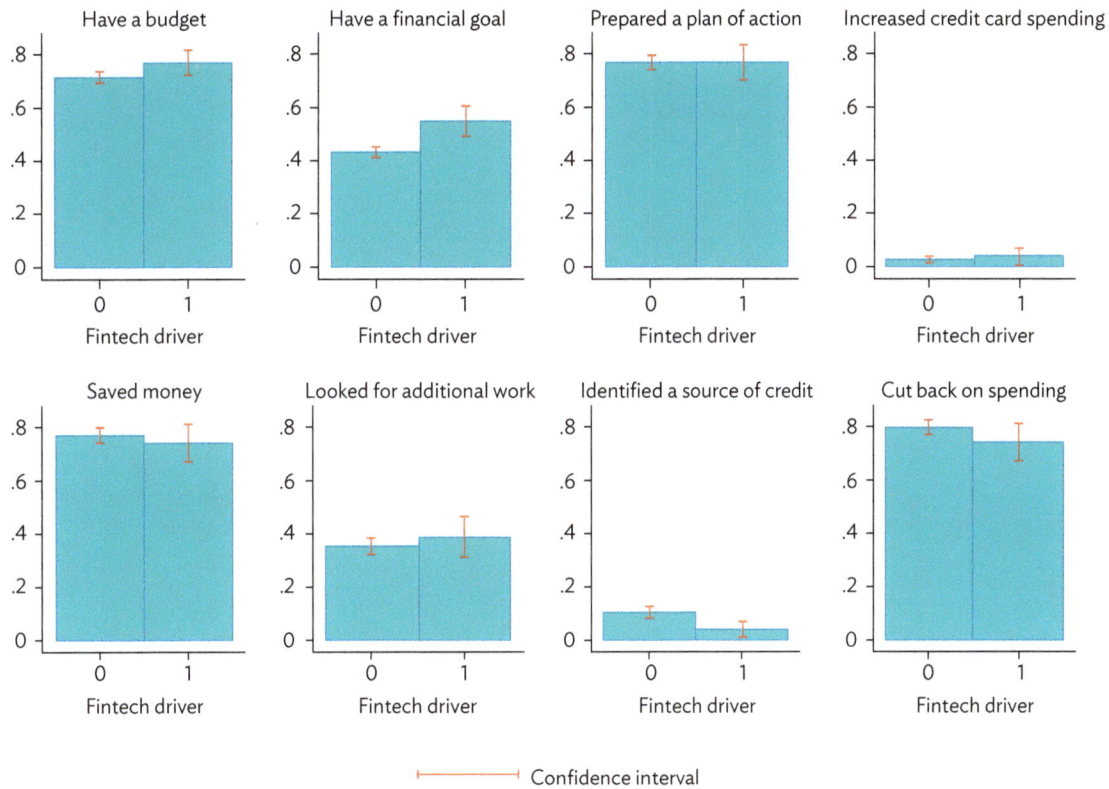

Note: The diagram plots the descriptive statistics of financial planning related variables between fintech and conventional drivers. The red vertical lines show the 95% confidence interval.

Source: Asian Development Bank.

We then investigated the driver's experience with basic financial instruments (Figure 10). First, we report the rate of ownership and usage of bank accounts, debit cards, credit cards, and use of online/mobile banking. Naturally, those without a bank account do not have access to other bank services. Financial inclusion, as measured by bank account ownership, is particularly low for the Philippines compared with other lower-middle-income countries. Among tricycle drivers, 23% had bank accounts, well below the Philippine average of 34.5% in 2017. Fintech drivers have a higher 29.5% rate, but still short of the nationwide average. This includes interest bearing accounts offered by mobile applications like commonly used GCash. Among bank account owners, 60% have a debit card, but only 5% have a credit card and 8% use online/mobile banking.

Higher account ownership among fintech drivers was linked to debit card ownership, but not to credit card and online or mobile banking. The debit card ownership rate was 19.8% for fintech drivers and 12.6% for conventional drivers, both below the average. But the 7-percentage point difference was consistent with the difference in account ownership. It is customary to issue a debit card when one opens a bank account. But it is an entirely different process and much more difficult to obtain a credit card. Hence, the ownership and use of credit cards were both negligible for each group. Few had any experience with online or mobile banking, which included online shopping.

Figure 10: Ownership of Financial Instruments

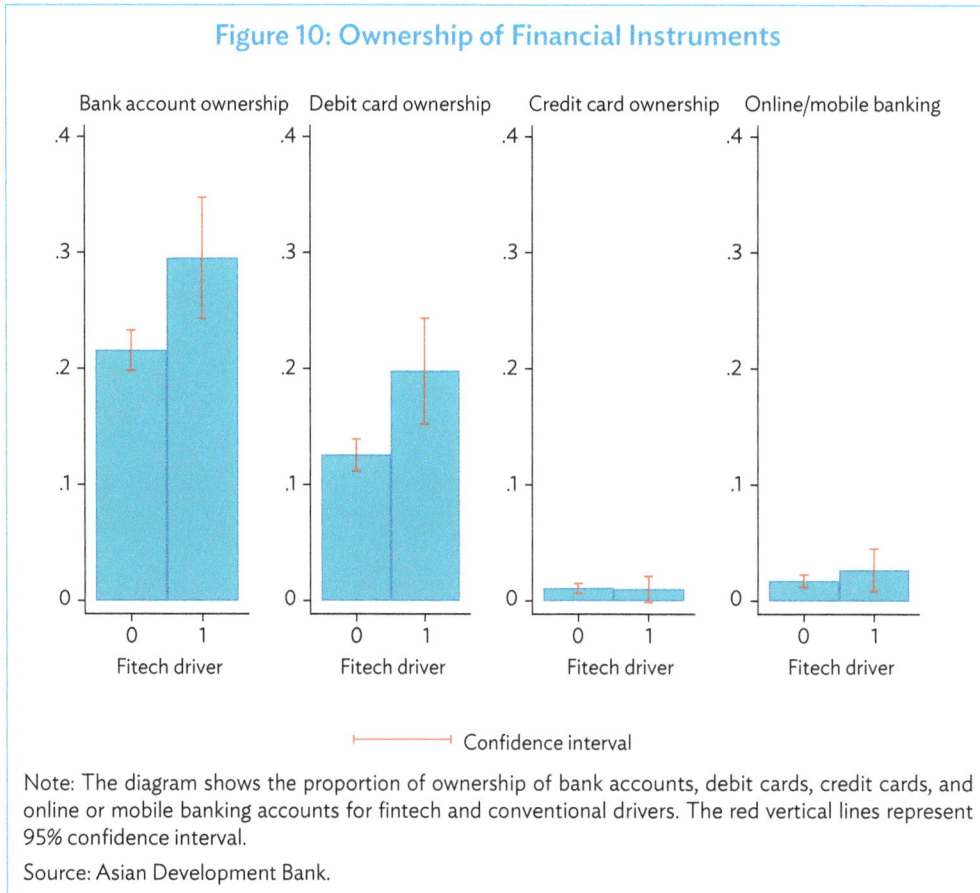

Note: The diagram shows the proportion of ownership of bank accounts, debit cards, credit cards, and online or mobile banking accounts for fintech and conventional drivers. The red vertical lines represent 95% confidence interval.

Source: Asian Development Bank.

Among drivers, 44% said they personally saved or set aside money for some reason or other (Table 12). A significantly higher number of fintech drivers had saved. They were 8.1 percentage points more likely to save than conventional drivers. As to why they saved, 19% said they saved for old age using instruments such as the Social Security Service (SSS), and 10% said they were saving to grow a business or a farm. There was no significant difference between fintech and conventional drivers in saving for old age, but fintech drivers were 10 percentage points more likely to save for business.

Another important question for financial inclusion is the choice of saving instrument. We include any type of savings (like cash at home) in our analysis. In a country with a developed and accessible financial system, people generally hold more savings in a formal financial institution and use cashless transactions more widely. The situation is quite different in the Philippines. While 33% said they were saving as cash at home, only 7% used an account at a formal financial institution. The difference between bank account ownership and usage suggests the existence of many dormant accounts. Instead of a formal account, drivers seem to resort more to informal savings groups, such as *paluwagan* and *kooperatiba*, with 10% of drivers using informal savings groups.

Table 12: Financial Instrument Ownership and Savings

Item	Total	Fintech (1)	Conventional (2)	Difference (1) – (2)
Bank account ownership	0.23	0.30	0.22	0.08**
	(0.42)	(0.46)	(0.41)	(0.03)
Debit card ownership	0.13	0.20	0.13	0.07**
	(0.34)	(0.40)	(0.33)	(0.02)
Credit card ownership	0.01	0.01	0.01	0.00
	(0.10)	(0.10)	(0.10)	(0.01)
Online/mobile banking	0.02	0.03	0.02	0.01
	(0.13)	(0.16)	(0.13)	(0.01)
Saved for some reason	0.44	0.51	0.43	0.08**
	(0.50)	(0.50)	(0.49)	(0.03)
Saved for old age	0.19	0.23	0.19	0.04
	(0.40)	(0.42)	(0.39)	(0.03)
Saved for business	0.10	0.18	0.09	0.09**
	(0.30)	(0.39)	(0.28)	(0.02)
Have cash/savings at home	0.33	0.37	0.32	0.05
	(0.47)	(0.48)	(0.47)	(0.03)
Have savings at financial institution	0.07	0.13	0.06	0.07**
	(0.25)	(0.34)	(0.23)	(0.02)
Have savings given to family members	0.07	0.08	0.06	0.02
	(0.25)	(0.28)	(0.24)	(0.02)
Have savings at informal savings group	0.10	0.15	0.09	0.06**
	(0.30)	(0.36)	(0.29)	(0.02)
Amount of savings in cash (pesos)	11,490	13,663	11,174	2,489
	(12892)	(13992)	(12706)	(1591)
Amount of savings at financial institution (pesos)	12,996	17,250	11,537	5712.9*
	(9831)	(10452)	(9242)	(2384)
Amount of savings through family members (pesos)	4,589	6,425	4,341	2,084
	(4406)	(4504)	(4359)	(1340)
Amount of savings at informal savings group (pesos)	10,463	12,754	9,999	2,755
	(7969)	(8223)	(7867)	(1706)
Have borrowed money	0.58	0.47	0.59	-0.12**
	(0.49)	(0.50)	(0.49)	(0.03)

continued on next page

Table 12 continued

Item	Total	Fintech (1)	Conventional (2)	Difference (1) – (2)
Borrowed for the purchase of property	0.02	0.02	0.02	0.00
	(0.14)	(0.15)	(0.14)	(0.01)
Borrowed for medical purpose	0.25	0.17	0.26	-0.09**
	(0.43)	(0.38)	(0.44)	(0.02)
Borrowed for business operation	0.03	0.04	0.03	0.01
	(0.17)	(0.19)	(0.17)	(0.01)
Observation	2,487	298	2,189	

Note: The table shows financial instrument ownership, saving by purpose, saving by instrument, savings amount, and borrowing by purpose among the entire sample of drivers, conventional drivers, and fintech drivers. Borrowing for business is limited to non-tricycle purposes. For each savings instrument, the average savings amount was calculated among those who reported a positive value, and to exclude outliers, the top 1% of saving amounts were dropped. Standard deviations are shown in parentheses below the mean. The last column shows the mean difference between the two groups ("Fintech" minus "Conventional"), and the standard error of difference is reported in parentheses. ** and * represent 5% and 1% significance, respectively.

Source: Asian Development Bank.

The average amount of savings is calculated among those who report positive savings amount for that specific savings instrument (Table 12). To exclude outliers that heavily affect the mean value, the top 1% of the savings distribution for each type is dropped before calculating the average. The result shows that the largest savings amount is at formal financial institutions, followed by cash savings at home and that in informal savings groups. Note that while only a handful of drivers use accounts at financial institutions, they store the largest amounts of savings.

Fintech drivers were more likely to use savings than conventional drivers. The difference was particularly significant for savings in financial institutions and informal savings groups. Savings amounts show a similar pattern. Fintech drivers were more likely to save a considerable sum of money in all types of saving methods. The differences were all significant at the 10% level except for savings via family members.

In terms of borrowing, 58% of drivers borrowed money from some source over the past 12 months. Note that all borrowings discussed in this section are restricted to non-tricycle purposes. Fintech drivers were 12 percentage points less likely to have a borrowing history. This could be due to already having a large tricycle loan. Among drivers with a borrowing history, most loans were for medical purposes. Only 2% of drivers borrowed for financing homes, apartments, or land, and 3% borrowed to operate a farm or business. One-quarter of the loans was for health or medical purposes. Fintech drivers, once again, borrowed less (9 percentage points lower).

Regression Analysis

So far, the descriptive statistics of drivers were discussed, and comparisons made between fintech drivers and conventional drivers. In this section, we use a multivariate linear regression to estimate the impact fintech has on the drivers' well-being. The purpose is to estimate how much access to fintech contributes to a rise in driver welfare, while controlling for various other factors that influence well-being. As controls, we consider demographic information, education and training, working behavior, and experimental measures. In addition, given that drivers show systematic differences in access to fintech loans across different TODAs, we also include TODA-specific fixed effects. This has an effect of controlling for all TODA-specific effects not included in our specification. One estimation specification is:

$$y_{ij} = \beta_0 + \beta_1 \, Fintech_{ij} + TODA_j + \beta_2 X_{ij} + \varepsilon_{ij} \text{---(1)}$$

The dependent variable is y_{ij} of driver i that belong to TODA j, and we consider all variables associated with a driver's well-being, financial planning, and accessibility. The list of dependent variables is shown in Table 13. The main explanatory variable of interest is the dummy variable $Fintech_{ij}$, which equals one if the driver i with TODA j availed of fintech loan. $TODA_j$ is a dummy variable for TODA j. X_{ij} is a vector of control variables. The list of control variables includes demographic information, schooling and vocational training, working behavior, cognitive abilities, and experimental measures. The detailed list of control variables is included in the Appendixes with their respective coefficients in the estimation. Lastly, ε_{ij} is a stochastic component with mean zero. The coefficient of interest is β_1. This captures the pure effect of a fintech loan on daily net salary and other outcome variables after controlling for all other information explained by control variables.

Even though a diverse set of control variables are included in the estimation, there always exists a probability that relevant information, usually unobservable variables, are omitted in the estimation process, which leads to a biased coefficient β_1. We alleviate the concern for omitted variable bias by including TODA-specific constant terms in each estimation. This effectively absorbs all variations across different TODAs and hence, we can compare drivers within TODAs between conventional and fintech drivers. TODA fixed effect terms will control all the TODA-specific information not included in our estimation specification. However, one caveat is that we only have a handful of TODAs where both conventional and fintech drivers are present. Therefore, a smaller number of samples can lead to less tightly estimated coefficients. The standard errors are clustered at the TODA level.

The estimation results are presented in Table 13. For each outcome variable, we run the regression with and without TODA fixed dummies. Panel A presents outcome variables associated with labor market activities. Consistent with comparison analysis, fintech loans significantly decrease working hours per day and increase working days per week. The total effect on working hours per week is negative, though the estimate is imprecisely estimated. Furthermore, fintech drivers also show shorter break times. All estimates become erratic and highly loosely estimated when TODA-specific terms are included.

Table 13: Estimation Result

Panel A Labor market activities	Working hours per day		Working days per week		Working hours per week		Break time in minutes	
	(1)	(2)	(3)	(4)	(5)	(6)	(7)	(8)
Fintech	-0.62**	0.29	0.14*	-0.05	-2.25	1.97	-11.29*	1.15
	(0.19)	(0.43)	(0.06)	(0.10)	(1.39)	(3.13)	(5.43)	(11.98)
Observation	2,465	2,465	2,465	2,465	2,465	2,465	2,465	2,465
Control variables	Yes	Yes	Yes	Yes	Yes	Yes	Yes	Yes
TODA fixed effect	No	Yes	No	Yes	No	Yes	No	Yes

continued on next page

Table 13 continued

Panel B Salary and income	Net salary per day		Driver income per month		Spouse income per month		Household income per month	
	(1)	(2)	(3)	(4)	(5)	(6)	(7)	(8)
Fintech	170.62**	107.09**	5,809**	3,856**	3,284**	3,364**	10,405**	15,307
	(17.74)	(40.43)	(666)	(1,382)	(738)	(1,120)	(2,692)	(10,830)
Observation	2,474	2,474	2,474	2,474	2,474	2,474	2,474	2,474
Control variables	Yes	Yes	Yes	Yes	Yes	Yes	Yes	Yes
TODA fixed effect	No	Yes	No	Yes	No	Yes	No	Yes

Panel C Repayment	Loan tenure in month		Total loan amount		Payment amount per week		Payment amount per month	
	(1)	(2)	(3)	(4)	(5)	(6)	(7)	(8)
Fintech	14.93**	11.06**	173,696**	142,426**	205**	191*	2,852**	2,032**
	(0.77)	(1.86)	(6,857)	(22,745)	(79)	(90)	(105)	(370)
Observation	1,080	1,080	1,079	1,079	324	324	978	978
Control variables	Yes	Yes	Yes	Yes	Yes	Yes	Yes	Yes
TODA fixed effect	No	Yes	No	Yes	No	Yes	No	Yes

Panel D Financial planning1	Have a budget		Have a financial goal		Prepared a plan		Increased credit card	
	(1)	(2)	(3)	(4)	(5)	(6)	(7)	(8)
Fintech	0.054*	0.065	0.136**	0.025	-0.006	-0.114	0.019	0.067
	(0.027)	(0.061)	(0.032)	(0.048)	(0.039)	(0.083)	(0.017)	(0.073)
Observation	2,473	2,473	2,474	2,474	1,103	1,103	1,103	1,103
Control variables	Yes	Yes	Yes	Yes	Yes	Yes	Yes	Yes
TODA fixed effect	No	Yes	No	Yes	No	Yes	No	Yes

Panel E Financial planning2	Saved/invested money		Looked for additional work		Identified a source of credit		Cut back on spending	
	(1)	(2)	(3)	(4)	(5)	(6)	(7)	(8)
Fintech	-0.016	0.183	-0.022	-0.044	-0.081**	-0.022	-0.083*	-0.126
	(0.040)	(0.124)	(0.042)	(0.142)	(0.023)	(0.055)	(0.039)	(0.102)
Observation	1,103	1,103	1,103	1,103	1,103	1,103	1,103	1,103
Control variables	Yes	Yes	Yes	Yes	Yes	Yes	Yes	Yes
TODA fixed effect	No	Yes	No	Yes	No	Yes	No	Yes

Panel F Financial accessibility	Bank account ownership		Debit card ownership		Credit card ownership		Online/mobile banking	
	(1)	(2)	(3)	(4)	(5)	(6)	(7)	(8)
Fintech	0.095**	-0.022	0.090**	0.03	0.000	0.002	0.012	0.03
	(0.028)	(0.077)	(0.024)	(0.059)	(0.007)	(0.017)	(0.010)	(0.023)
Observation	2,474	2,474	2,474	2,474	2,474	2,474	2,474	2,474
Control variables	Yes	Yes	Yes	Yes	Yes	Yes	Yes	Yes
TODA fixed effect	No	Yes	No	Yes	No	Yes	No	Yes

continued on next page

Table 13 continued

Panel G Saving1	Saved for some reason		Saved for old age		Saved for business	
	(1)	(2)	(3)	(4)	(5)	(6)
Fintech	0.077*	−0.044	0.048	0.05	0.074**	0.043
	(0.032)	(0.073)	(0.026)	(0.057)	(0.023)	(0.063)
Observation	2,474	2,474	2,474	2,474	2,474	2,474
Control variables	Yes	Yes	Yes	Yes	Yes	Yes
TODA fixed effect	No	Yes	No	Yes	No	Yes

Panel H Saving2	Have cash/ savings at home		Have savings at financial institution		Have savings through family members		Have savings at informal savings group	
	(1)	(2)	(3)	(4)	(5)	(6)	(7)	(8)
Fintech	0.039	−0.061	0.078**	0.057	0.02	−0.004	0.049*	0.039
	(0.031)	(0.072)	(0.020)	(0.037)	(0.017)	(0.045)	(0.022)	(0.044)
Observation	2,474	2,474	2,474	2,474	2,474	2,474	2,474	2,474
Control variables	Yes	Yes	Yes	Yes	Yes	Yes	Yes	Yes
TODA fixed effect	No	Yes	No	Yes	No	Yes	No	Yes

Panel I Saving3	Savings in cash		Savings at financial institution		Savings through family members		Savings at informal savings group	
	(1)	(2)	(3)	(4)	(5)	(6)	(7)	(8)
Fintech	2994	403	18,275*	36,249	5,704	−12,078	3,081	2,239
	(1,994)	(6,787)	(8,943)	(39,594)	(4,134)	(9,636)	(3,506)	(6,114)
Observation	688	688	125	125	127	127	222	222
Control variables	Yes	Yes	Yes	Yes	Yes	Yes	Yes	Yes
TODA fixed effect	No	Yes	No	Yes	No	Yes	No	Yes

Panel J Borrowing	Have borrowed money		Borrowed for property purchase		Borrowed for medical purpose		Borrowed for business operation	
	(1)	(2)	(3)	(4)	(5)	(6)	(7)	(8)
Fintech	−0.119**	−0.146*	−0.003	−0.021	−0.103**	−0.097	0.009	−0.007
	(0.032)	(0.075)	(0.011)	(0.019)	(0.026)	(0.062)	(0.012)	(0.025)
Observation	2,474	2,474	2,474	2,474	2,474	2,474	2,474	2,474
Control variables	Yes	Yes	Yes	Yes	Yes	Yes	Yes	Yes
TODA fixed effect	No	Yes	No	Yes	No	Yes	No	Yes

TODA = tricycle operators and drivers' association.

Note: The table shows estimation results of the impact of fintech loan on driver daily net salaries, financial planning variables, financial accessibility, and savings associated variables. All estimations control for demographic information, schooling and training, working behavior, cognitive abilities, and experimental measures. The independent variable of interest is a fintech dummy indicating whether one has availed of a fintech loan. Odd numbered columns do not include TODA fixed effect terms, while even numbered columns include them. Standard errors are reported in parentheses. For estimation with TODA fixed effect, standard errors are clustered at TODA level. ** and * represent 5% and 1% significance, respectively.

Source: Asian Development Bank.

Panel B lists outcome variables related to salary and income. One can easily see that fintech loans leads to a considerable increase in daily net salary and monthly income. The estimates are economically and statistically significant. This implies that even after accounting for differences in demographic and socioeconomic characteristics, fintech drivers still show even larger salaries and income. Estimates are robust to including TODA-specific terms and are tightly estimated. This gives confidence to our prior result that fintech loans boost a driver's overall income.

Panel C presents a driver's repayment activities. Four variables are considered: loan tenure, total loan amount, and regular payment amount in weeks and months. Once again, the result show that fintech drivers have significantly larger repayment responsibilities. They are obligated to pay larger sums over longer periods. The weekly payment amount shown in columns 5 and 6 is estimated among weekly payers only. The monthly payment amount shown in columns 7 and 8 is estimated among both weekly and monthly payers, after adjusting weekly amounts to monthly levels. This is to increase the sample size given that conventional and fintech drivers mainly use different repayment frequencies. All are tightly estimated and are robust to accounting for TODA-specific effects.

Panels D and E display variables regarding a driver's financial planning behavior. We are interested in how novel loans can induce a change in a driver's daily habit of managing money and achieving financial goals. Consistent with comparison analysis, the estimates suggest that fintech loans induce drivers to keep a budget and have financial goals. We also examine actions taken to achieve the goals. As suggested earlier, fintech drivers are less likely to identify a source of credit, probably due to their already large vehicle loan. They are also less likely to cut back on spending. Inclusion of TODA fixed effect terms absorbs most of the variations in the data and coefficients mostly turn insignificant.

Panel F reports the results on financial accessibility. We specifically consider ownership of bank accounts at a formal financial institution, debit cards, credit cards, and experience with online/mobile banking. The coefficients estimated are consistent with the prior analysis that fintech loans lead to higher bank account and debit card ownership. However, they have negligible effect on credit card ownership and experience with online/mobile banking. All estimates turn statistically indistinguishable from zero once TODA-specific terms are included.

The impact of fintech loans on savings behavior and savings amount are displayed in Panels G to I. It is easily seen that estimation results are largely unchanged from the comparison analysis. Fintech loans cause more drivers to save and especially save for business operations. Examining savings instruments also reveals that fintech induces more savings through formal financial institutions and informal savings groups. The estimates are positive and significant for these outcome variables, as shown in Panel H columns 3 and 7. Savings amounts are also shown to be, in general, insensitive to fintech loans except savings at financial institutions. This makes it clear that fintech loans indeed cause more people to open a bank account and deposit larger amounts. We also check to see if this is a result of crowding out savings through any other instrument, but we could not find any evidence that fintech loans lead to a decrease in savings for any savings means. The inclusion of TODA fixed effect terms leads to large standard errors and most of the coefficients are highly loosely estimated.

Lastly, Panel J presents the effect of fintech loans on borrowing behavior through regression analysis. The novel loan leads to a smaller probability of borrowing for non-tricycle purposes. This is probably because of large auto-loans and hence the crowding out of borrowing for other reasons. Examination of borrowing for specific purposes reveals that auto-loans crowd out borrowing for medical purposes, but hardly has any effect on borrowing for the purchase of property and for business operations. This is consistent with the simple comparison analysis.

(ii) Impact of Fintech on Regional Economic Development

It is too early to determine the impact fintech has on regional economic development. The new financing method of using IoT technology has only recently been introduced and the number of users is not enough to assess the regional impact. Hence, we discuss some of the potential effects and mechanisms through which new fintech can affect regional development.

Several development economics papers document the importance of financial institutions for economic development (Arestis and Demetriades 1997; Beck, Levine, and Loayza 2000; Bencivenga and Smith 1991; Benhabib and Spiegel 2000). Capital accumulation and allocation facilitated by financial intermediaries provide credit to businesses for investment, thereby fostering regional economic growth. Banks, or any type of financial intermediary, assess the creditworthiness of customers to price loans—taking into account credit history, collateral, working status, and so forth. However, there are asymmetric information, agency problems, and high monitoring costs that cause inefficient allocation of funds. This results in households and firms, especially small ones, facing a funding gap (Klagge and Martin, 2005). The contribution financial institutions offer economic growth is through screening and monitoring. They facilitate the efficient allocation of funds to households and firms. Our auto-loan works in a similar fashion. The new fintech here reduces the requirement of loan applicants, in our case prospective drivers, by alleviating moral hazard and enforcement of payment problems. Using IoT technology, they can constantly monitor the working behavior of their client drivers and hence, relieve the moral hazard problem. And, in case of delinquency, they can easily confiscate the motorcycle and retrieve some value from their nonperforming loan. This allows more efficient enforcement of payment. By making the auto-loan more accessible to customers, it helps generate new drivers and promotes the tricycle market.

The significance of the technology lies in more than just alleviating a driver's liquidity constraints. It also provides a stepping stone to wider opportunities for the poor. After completing the fintech loan, the regular repayments made to the fintech company can be used as a credit history that opens opportunities for clients to access formal financial institutions like commercial banks. With a payment record, they are more likely to qualify for a larger loan from commercial banks for career advancement and to make larger investments. Former tricycle drivers can take advantage of this opportunity to potentially becoming Grab or taxi drivers in the Philippines.

The next potential mechanism through which fintech can contribute to regional development is by promoting financial inclusion. The comparison analysis between fintech and conventional drivers shows the possible beneficial effects of GMS loans in inducing clients to open a bank account, keep a household budget, and increase savings, especially through formal financial accounts. Again, it is unclear whether the analysis points to self-selection or the effect of the fintech loan. However, given that fintech drivers outperform drivers with dealer financing other than GMS, it suggests that the new technology is in some way causing drivers to lead a more frugal lifestyle with higher savings, planned expenditures, and greater involvement in financial institutions. It could be that GMS approvals require these factors. Regardless of how fintech drivers performed better in planning expenditures and saving more through financial institutions, it is clear fintech is conducive to regional economic development.

(iii) Potential Challenges to Maximizing Fintech Benefits

The fintech loan combined with new IoT technology allows wider access to vehicle loans. While theoretically true, it does not guarantee success to motorcycle dealers adopting this new method. Widening windows of opportunity also means that customers with slightly less capacity to repay will also qualify for loans. It boils down to whether the technology helps making more loans that are properly repaid. Given the comparison analysis that showed longer loan tenures, larger loan amounts, and larger regular payment amounts, it is true that fintech drivers face larger and stricter repayment obligations. Whether the technology induces drivers to bear the responsibility and more successfully complete repayment schedules than other dealer companies will determine the technology's effectiveness.

The questions on driver behavior and repayment shed light on the repayment challenges facing drivers. We asked drivers (i) if they experienced any problems in repaying the loan, and if so, which problems they encountered, and (ii) if there was any instance where they missed paying on time over the past 6 months, and if so, what happened afterward. Here, we compare the responses between fintech drivers and drivers from other motorcycle dealers (Table 14). First, a significantly higher percentage of fintech drivers had problems paying loans—43% reported problems compared with 31% of conventional drivers. As to specific types of problems, there was a slightly different pattern. Most problems on repayment were due to busy work schedules or more important cash needs. However, the main difference was that while other dealer clients reported problems that were more the "customer's fault," in the sense that drivers failed to prepare enough money to pay on time, fintech drivers problems were more systemic. They showed a higher percentage of problems like dealers not recording a driver's payment properly or a payment not remitted by the collector.

Fintech drivers were significantly more likely to have missed a payment during the past 6 months. The two types of dealers had completely different responses. Dealers usually punished drivers by adjusting payment amounts, with drivers either having to pay a one-time fee or their regular payment amounts were adjusted. On the other hand, GMS rarely used such policies. Instead, they would simply shut down and confiscate the tricycle—a more severe penalty. Although we do not have data on instances of confiscated motorcycle reclaimed after paying arrears, the data seem to suggest drivers were hurt more when failing to repay. Given that more fintech drivers complained about the inattention of dealers and collectors to meticulously record repayment, this potentially hurt drivers more.

In short, the data suggest that although fintech loans open new opportunities to expand business and contribute to poverty reduction, the challenge of inducing clients to keep to repayment schedules and maintain good track of payment records remains. The technology allows the harsh penalties of impounding the motorcycle remotely, but does not act as a positive incentive to work harder or repay the debt. This is where innovation is required to better take advantage of the benefits the technology has to offer.

Table 14: Repayment Problems and Consequences of Missing Payments

Item	Fintech (1)	Other dealers (2)	Difference (1) - (2)
Experienced problem in repayment	0.43	0.31	0.12**
	(0.50)	(0.46)	(0.03)
Reasons why payment could not be made			
Busy schedule/sickness	0.41	0.62	-0.2**
	(0.49)	(0.49)	(0.06)
More important use of money	0.39	0.45	-0.06
	(0.49)	(0.50)	(0.06)

continued on next page

Table 14 continued

Item	Fintech (1)	Other dealers (2)	Difference (1) - (2)
Office of the payment center is far away	0.02	0.01	0.01
	(0.15)	(0.10)	(0.02)
Forgot the due date	0.03	0.36	-0.33**
	(0.17)	(0.48)	(0.04)
Payment not recorded by the dealer	0.15	0.01	0.13**
	(0.36)	(0.12)	(0.03)
Payment not remitted by the collector	0.02	0.01	0.01
	(0.12)	(0.10)	(0.01)
Missed paying dues on time	0.48	0.29	0.19**
	(0.50)	(0.45)	(0.03)
What happens afterward			
Nothing happens	0.09	0.23	-0.14**
	(0.29)	(0.42)	(0.04)
Tricycle is shut down	0.76	0.09	0.67**
	(0.43)	(0.29)	(0.04)
Receive a warning	0.17	0.13	0.04
	(0.38)	(0.33)	(0.04)
Receive a one-time penalty	0.02	0.38	-0.35**
	(0.14)	(0.49)	(0.04)
Regular payment amount increases	0.03	0.28	-0.25**
	(0.18)	(0.45)	(0.04)
Collector calls to demands payment	0.09	0.10	0.00
	(0.29)	(0.29)	(0.03)
Observation	298	655	

Note: The table reports whether drivers experienced any problem in repayment, and if so why it could not be made. It also reports whether the drivers missed paying on time in the past 6 months and if so, what happened afterward. The results are shown for fintech drivers and drivers who borrowed from dealers other than GMS. Standard deviations are shown in parentheses below the mean. The last column shows the mean difference between the two groups ("Fintech" minus "Other dealers"), and the standard error of difference is reported in parentheses. ** and * represent 5% and 1% significance, respectively.

Source: Asian Development Bank.

7. A Financing Model for the Self-Employed: Implications from the Survey and COVID-19

In the Philippines, MSMEs play a critical role in driving the national economy. They accounted for 99.5% of enterprises and 63.2% of the employed labor force in 2018 (latest available data) (ADB, 2020a). More than 80% of MSMEs are engaged in services, especially distributive trade. Access to finance is a chronic barrier to MSME survival and growth. Bank credit to MSMEs accounted for 6.1% of total bank loans in 2019—a single-digit percentage share since 2013.

MSMEs are roughly classified into two types: stability- and growth-oriented firms. Stability-oriented firms include slow or zero growth wholesale and retail trade, family-run or home businesses, and sole proprietorships or the self-employed with small-scale routine operations—the tricycle drivers covered in this report are considered this type. They are the flip side of the growth-oriented firms that include technology-based MSMEs, young entrepreneurs, and start-ups seeking business growth with innovative mind.

The scale and objective of funding for the two types differ. Stability-oriented firms generally seek short-term and small amounts of working capital to survive their daily business and rely mostly on their own capital and informal sources—including borrowing from family, relatives, friends, local communities, and moneylenders (Shinozaki, 2012). Growth-oriented firms look for longer-term and larger amounts of growth capital to expand business. They seek access to broader financing options—including bank credit, capital markets, and digital financial services such as peer-to-peer lending and equity crowdfunding.

The coronavirus disease (COVID-19) significantly altered peoples' lives and business activities, causing huge problems in raising enough working capital to retain business operations during the pandemic, especially for stability-oriented smaller firms. Most businesses in the Philippines are smaller firms and the self-employed. They were forced to temporary close of business or faced a sharp drop in sales and revenue. Demand for their products and services decreased. And they faced supply disruptions; all affected by the pandemic and associated quarantine measures, which included lockdowns (ADB, 2020b and 2020c). The pandemic impact appeared at different times for micro, small, and medium-sized enterprises, respectively, depending on their ability to cope with the impact. Smaller firms and the self-employed faced a more serious lack of funds. However, their funding attitude has not changed, though government offered several financial assistance programs in response to the pandemic, they still relied on informal financing sources.

The COVID-19 crisis has accelerated the shift toward digital transactions across all businesses. Smaller firms and the self-employed are not exempt from this trend. They have also had to adapt, even if their businesses generally require personal contact. Conventional MSMEs are generally unfamiliar with digital transactions. During the pandemic, most initially did not use digital finance platforms to obtain working capital. But the digital transformation is inevitable for businesses operating under a new normal that promotes a more contactless society. This movement also affects the tricycle driving market. ADB's rapid MSME survey in the Philippines conducted in March–April 2020 revealed that some MSMEs transferred employment to other businesses, suggesting that some tricycle drivers moved on to other types of business, such as the food delivery services that enjoyed higher demand during the pandemic.

Key findings from the baseline survey of tricycle drivers hold several implications on financing models for the self-employed. As the survey was conducted in 2019, its analysis on the impact of fintech loans to tricycle drivers was pre-COVID-19. But the results emphasized the importance of fintech for the self-employed—like tricycle drivers—in making it through the pandemic and maintaining a new normalcy.

The comparison between fintech and conventional drivers showed fintech drivers have more risk appetite, rationalize their working hours more, and earn much higher income than conventional drivers. They have relatively higher access to financing sources with good financial plans and goals, while facing a large obligation to loan repayments. Bank account ownership (with debit card) is higher among fintech drivers, but credit card and mobile banking as well as online shopping are not often used. They save, but mostly using cash-at-home and through informal savings groups; few use formal financial institutions to save. The regression analysis indicated that fintech loans intensify driver work habits. They work more days per week, boost overall income, improve money management, have financial goals, and create more savings for business operations. While the loan repayment burden reduces their incentive to borrow for non-tricycle purposes, fintech loans allow more people to open bank accounts. Overall, the survey findings suggest that fintech improves tricycle drivers' living standards and social welfare—and potentially support development of regional economies by enhancing financial inclusion.

Fintech loans based on the IoT device as such provided by GMS is promising to enhance financial access for the self-employed or sole proprietorships—especially those in transportation and logistics—and to ensure their business survives under the new normal with improved living standards and social welfare. Constant monitoring of repayment condition as well as working behavior using the IoT device will enable lenders to mitigate borrowers' asymmetric information and allow the borrower to access more readily working capital. This will benefit particular business sectors of the self-employed such as transportation, logistics, and delivery services. The survey findings suggest that, through fintech loans, they can enjoy a more frugal lifestyle with higher savings and planned expenditures, and can open accounts in financial institutions. Familiarity with fintech loans or digital financial services will stimulate more e-commerce and entice a digital transformation of their business to fit new business modalities in a post-COVID-19 world.

Nonetheless, there remain several challenges to promoting fintech loans or digital financial services for the self-employed, such as tricycle drivers. The surveyed drivers with fintech loans tend to hesitate when accessing new loans due to the large repayment burden on ongoing tricycle loans. But they are relatively good at financial planning and goal setting. If they receive appropriate business advice and development services, they may qualify for other types of fintech loans and increase access to formal financial services.

Financial education is an essential component to promoting digital financial services for the self-employed or sole proprietorships. It allows them to better understand loan conditions and value-additions to their business (and lifestyle) by accessing technology-based loans. According to the baseline survey, less than 10% of drivers were aware of their loan interest rates, suggesting the majority of drivers do not understand how loans work. This may increase default risk among tricycle drivers; they need the appropriate knowledge on financial instruments, including digital finance, which they can learn through training programs by government, private sector, or financial institutions. The tricycle drivers surveyed were mostly male, but to a certain extent, spouses or female partners drove decision-making on how money was used. Financial education and training involves both business owners and their life partners.

Designing a fintech loan that satisfies the demand and business/life conditions of the self-employed is key for promoting digital financial services to them. The survey found that fintech loans we analyzed penalize drivers more severely than other dealer financing schemes, for example, simply confiscating the tricycle rather than adjusting loan tenure and repayment amounts. Low-income households or the self-employed worry about their unstable income and expenditures for future life events. This leads to a cash-based economy. Financial products must be adapted to respond better to real-life needs so people are persuaded to use new financial tools like digital financial services or fintech loans.

8. Moving Forward

The study concludes that fintech improves living standards and the social welfare of tricycle drivers (self-employed), and supports development of the country's local economies through enhanced financial inclusion. The study suggests that fintech loans incentivize driver work habits with more regular working days, higher incomes, and improved fund management ability with financial planning, and create more savings for business operations. Consequently, fintech loans can stimulate more people to open bank accounts, contributing to further financial inclusion.

COVID-19 triggered a shift of MSME business models from conventional ways with personal contact to more contactless digital transactions. The tricycle driving industry thrives on community-based markets in the Philippines and may not fully meld into digital transformation—due to the nature of its business. However, mobile-based ride-hailing services modeled on the Singapore-based Grab and the Philippine-based Angkas may allow for increased digital operations of the tricycle driving industry post-COVID-19. But they need to demonstrate they can safely work under the new normal—for example, placing partitions in the client compartment with obligatory customer face masks and/or face shields. To customize their tricycles to protect customers from the virus, they may need additional funding. But community-based lending and informal financing that they popularly use are always accompanied by physical contacts. Given the high penetration of smartphones among tricycle drivers, it would be a good opportunity to promote fintech loans and other digital financial services for drivers—including savings and insurance—under the new normal. To this end, financial education or financial literacy training including digital finance is critical for drivers to access more new financial tools with more appropriate knowledge and better understanding of their benefits. Given that most tricycle drivers are male, financial literacy training should include their wives and female partners as they have certain decision-making power over household budgets. Financial education will also cultivate a new customer base or risk takers for fintech loans and the digital finance industry.

The COVID-19 crisis have also caused a job shift among tricycle drivers to other types of businesses, such as food delivery and mobile-based ride-hailing services due to the restricted operations of tricycle driving caused by the pandemic and associated quarantine measures. A follow-up study on how business and the lives of tricycle drivers have changed from the pre- to post-COVID-19 era would be worth consideration.

References

Afriat, S. N. 1972. "Efficiency estimation of production functions." *International economic review*: 568–598.

Agarwal, S., S. Alok, P. Ghosh, and S. Gupta. 2019. *Fintech and Credit Scoring for the Millennials: Evidence using Mobile and Social Footprints*. Available at SSRN 3507827.

Arestis, P. and P. Demetriades. 1997. "Financial development and economic growth: assessing the evidence." *The economic journal*, 107(442): 783–799.

Armendáriz de Aghion, B. 1999. Development banking. *Journal of Development Economics*, 58(1):83–100.

Armendáriz de Aghion, B. and C. Gollier. 2000. "Peer group formation in an adverse selection model." *Economic Journal*, 110(465):632–643.

Armendáriz de Aghion, B. and J. Morduch. 2010. *The Economics of Microfinance, Second Edition*. Cambridge, Mass.: MIT Press.

Asian Development Bank (ADB). 2020a. *Asia Small and Medium-Sized Enterprise Monitor 2020: Volume I–Country and Regional Reviews*. Manila: ADB.

ADB. 2020b. *Asia Small and Medium-Sized Enterprise Monitor 2020: Volume II–COVID-19 Impact on Micro, Small, and Medium-Sized Enterprises in Developing Asia*. Manila: ADB.

ADB. 2020c. *The COVID-19 Impact on Philippine Business: Key Findings from the Enterprise Survey*. Manila: ADB.

Ayyagari, M., A. Demirgüç-Kunt, and V. Maksimovic. 2014. "Who creates jobs in developing countries?" *Small Business Economics* 43: 75-99.

Ayyagari, M, T. Beck, and A. Demirgüç-Kunt. 2007. "Small and Medium Enterprises across the Globe." *Small Business Economics*, 29(4): 415-434

Banerjee, A. V., T. Besley, and T.W. Guinnane. 1994. "Thy neighbor's keeper: The design of a credit cooperative with theory and a test." *Quarterly Journal of Economics*, 109(2): 491–515.

Banerjee, A., E. Duflo, R. Glennerster, and C. Kinnan. 2015. "The miracle of microfinance? Evidence from a randomized evaluation." *American Economic Journal: Applied Economics*, 7(1): 22-53.

Banerjee, A., D. Karlan, and J. Zinman. 2015. "Six Randomized Evaluations of Microcredit: Introduction and Further Steps". *American Economic Journal: Applied Economics*, 7 (1): 1-21.

Beck, T., A. Demirgüç-Kunt, and V. Maksimovic. 2005. "Financial and legal constraints to growth: does firm size matter?" *The Journal of finance*, 60(1): 137-177.

Beck, T., R. Levine, and N. Loayza. 2000. "Finance and the Sources of Growth." *Journal of financial economics*, 58(1-2): 261-300.

Beck, T., H. Pamuk, R. Ramrattan, and B. R. Uras. 2018. "Payment instruments, finance and development." *Journal of Development Economics*, 133:162-186.

Bencivenga, V. R. and B.D. Smith. 1991. "Financial intermediation and endogenous growth." *The review of economic studies*, 58(2): 195-209.

Benhabib, J. and M.M. Spiegel. 2000. "The role of financial development in growth and investment." *Journal of economic growth*, 5(4): 341-360.

Berg, T., V. Burg, A. Gombović, and M. Puri. 2018. *On the rise of fintechs–credit scoring using digital footprints* (No. w24551). National Bureau of Economic Research.

Besley, T. and S. Coate. 1995. "Group lending, repayment incentives and social collateral." *Journal of Development Economics*, 46(1): 1–18.

Blumenstock, J. E., N. Eagle, and M. Fafchamps. 2016. "Airtime transfers and mobile communications: Evidence in the aftermath of natural disasters." *Journal of Development Economics*, 120: 157-181.

Bruhn, M., D. Karlan, and A. Schoar. 2010. "What capital is missing in developing countries?" *American Economic Review*, 100(2): 629-633.

Cho, Y., and M. Honorati. 2014. "Entrepreneurship programs in developing countries: A meta regression analysis." *Labour Economics*, 28: 110-130.

Choi, S., R. Fisman, D. Gale, and S. Kariv. 2007. "Consistency and heterogeneity of individual behavior under uncertainty." *American economic review*, 97(5): 1921-1938.

Demirgüç-Kunt, A. and V. Maksimovic. 1998. "Law, finance, and firm growth." *The Journal of Finance*, 53(6): 2107–2137.

Frame, W. S., A. Srinivasan, and L. Woosley. 2001. "The effect of credit scoring on small-business lending." *Journal of money, credit and banking*: 813-825.

Field, E., R. Pande, J. Papp, and N. Rigol. 2013. "Does the classic microfinance model discourage entrepreneurship among the poor? Experimental evidence from India." *American Economic Review*, 103(6): 2196-2226.

Gangopadhyay, S., M Ghatak, and R. Lensink. 2005. "Joint liability lending and the peer selection effect." *Economic Journal*, 115(506): 1005–1015.

Ghatak, M. 1999. "Group lending, local information and peer selection." *Journal of Development Economics*, 60: 27–50.

Giné, X., and D.S. Karlan. 2014. "Group versus individual liability: Short and long term evidence from Philippine microcredit lending groups." *Journal of Development Economics*, 107: 65–83.

Gosavi, A. 2018. "Can mobile money help firms mitigate the problem of access to finance in Eastern sub-Saharan Africa?" *Journal of African Business*, 19(3): 343-360.

Guttman, J. M. 2008. "Assortative matching, adverse selection, and group lending." *Journal of Development Economics*, 87(1): 51–56.

Hoff, K. and J. E. Stiglitz. 199. "Introduction: Imperfect information and rural credit markets: Puzzles and policy perspectives." *The World Bank Economic Review*, 4(3): 235-250.

Jack, W. and T. Suri. 2014. "Risk sharing and transactions costs: Evidence from Kenya›s mobile money revolution." *American Economic Review*, 104(1): 183-223.

Karlan, D. and M. Valdivia. 2011. "Teaching entrepreneurship: Impact of business training on microfinance clients and institutions." *Review of Economics and Statistics*, 93(2): 510-527.

Karlan, D. and J. Zinman. 2009. "Observing Unobservables: Identifying information asymmetries with a consumer credit field experiment." *Econometrica*, 77(6): 1993–2008.

Karlan, D. and J. Zinman. 2010. "Expanding credit access: Using randomized supply decisions to estimate the impacts." *The Review of Financial Studies*, 23(1): 433-464.

Klagge, B. and R. Martin. 2005. "Decentralized versus centralized financial systems: Is there a case for local capital markets?" *Journal of Economic Geography*, 5(4): 387-421.

Levine, R. 1999. *Financial development and economic growth: views and agenda*. The World Bank.

McKenzie, D. 2020. "Small business training to improve management practices in developing countries: Reassessing the evidence for 'training doesn't work'." *Oxford Review of Economic Policy*, forthcoming.

Munyegera, G. K. and T. Matsumoto. 2016. "Mobile money, remittances, and household welfare: panel evidence from rural Uganda." *World Development*, 79: 127-137.

Prediger, S. and G. Gut. 2014. "Microcredit and business-training programs: Effective strategies for micro-and small enterprise growth?" *GIGA Focus*, Number 3.

Rajan, R. G. and L. Zingales. 1996. *Financial dependence and growth (No. w5758)*. National bureau of economic research.

Riley, E. 2018. 'Mobile money and risk sharing against village shocks." *Journal of Development Economics*, 135: 43-58.

Shapiro, D. 2019. *Limited Impact of Business Development Programs on Entrepreneurs' Profitability in the Presence of Ambiguity Aversion*. Available at SSRN 3410192.

Shinozaki, S. 2012. A New Regime of SME Finance in Emerging Asia: Empowering Growth-Oriented SMEs to Build Resilient National Economies. *ADB Working Paper Series on Regional Economic Integration*. No.104. Manila: ADB.

Stiglitz, J. E. 1990. "Peer monitoring and credit market." *World Bank Economic Review*, 4(3): 351–366.

Suri, T. 2017. "Mobile money." *Annual Review of Economics*, 9: 497-520.

Suri, T., W. Jack, and T. M. Stoker. 2012. "Documenting the birth of a financial economy." *Proceedings of the National Academy of Sciences*, 109(26): 10,257-10,262.

Van Tassel, E. 1999. 'Group lending under asymmetric information." *Journal of Development Economics* 60(1): 3–25.

Appendixes

1. List of Control Variables Used in Regression Analysis

Demographic variables:

- Male: dummy variable indicating male drivers
- Married: dummy variable indicating married drivers
- Age: age of drivers in 2019
- Age2: age squared
- Exp: experience of working as a tricycle driver in years
- Exp2: experience squared
- Same province: dummy variable indicating whether one has always lived in the same province
- Health: categorical variable indicating current physical health status using the scale 1 = "Very good", 2 = "Good", 3 = "Moderate", 4 = "Bad" and 5 = "Very bad"
- HH member: number of household members including the driver

Schooling and training:

- Education: year of schooling
- Training: dummy variable indicating whether one has received any type of vocational training
- Motivation: categorical variable indicating the degree of motivation to work hard using the scale 1 = "Strongly agree", 2 = "Agree", 3 = "Neither disagree nor agree", 4 = "Disagree" and 5 = "Strongly disagree"

Working behavior:

- Past job: dummy variable indicating whether one had any type of past job
- Second job: dummy variable indicating whether one has a second job

Cognitive abilities and experimental measures:

- Score_raven: score from 4 questions on Raven's test
- Score_numeracy: score from 8 questions on numeracy
- Score_ financial: score from 10 questions on financial literacy
- Risk preference: risk preference measure computed from 20 questions in risk preference experiments
- Impatience: impatience measure computed from 30 questions in time preference experiments
- CCEI_risk: Critical Cost Efficiency Index calculated from 20 questions in risk preference experiments
- CCEI_time: Critical Cost Efficiency Index calculated from 30 questions in time preference experiments

2. Regression Tables including Full Set of Control Variables

Table A1: Estimation Result with Full Set of Controls

Panel A	Working hours per day		Working days per week		Working hours per week		Break time in minutes	
	(1)	(2)	(3)	(4)	(5)	(6)	(7)	(8)
Fintech	-0.617**	0.289	0.139*	(0.046)	(2.250)	1.970	-11.29*	1.153
	(0.192)	(0.430)	(0.059)	(0.104)	(1.394)	(3.132)	(5.429)	(11.980)
Male	0.444	0.626	0.160	0.242	4.969	6.701*	23.580	23.130
	(0.528)	(0.493)	(0.166)	(0.149)	(3.725)	(3.147)	(13.700)	(14.360)
Married	0.062	0.115	0.023	0.075	0.754	1.644	0.111	-2.211
	(0.165)	(0.177)	(0.054)	(0.059)	(1.210)	(1.259)	(4.841)	(5.490)
Age	0.0881*	0.0804*	0.0287*	0.025	0.890**	0.769*	2.234	3.514**
	(0.039)	(0.041)	(0.012)	(0.013)	(0.279)	(0.301)	(1.149)	(1.269)
Age2	-0.00134**	-0.00125**	-0.000345*	0.000	-0.0123**	-0.0109**	-0.021	-0.0368*
	(0.000)	(0.000)	(0.000)	(0.000)	(0.003)	(0.003)	(0.013)	(0.015)
Exp	0.0627**	0.0488*	-0.003	0.003	0.337*	0.323*	-0.329	-0.733
	(0.019)	(0.023)	(0.006)	(0.007)	(0.139)	(0.161)	(0.612)	(0.743)
Exp2	-0.00149**	-0.00123*	0.000	0.000	-0.00762*	-0.007	0.009	0.019
	(0.000)	(0.001)	(0.000)	(0.000)	(0.004)	(0.004)	(0.018)	(0.019)
Same province	-0.362**	-0.176	0.053	-0.027	-1.588	-1.348	-2.002	-3.411
	(0.126)	(0.159)	(0.039)	(0.045)	(0.920)	(1.157)	(3.830)	(4.745)
Health	-0.114	-0.129	-0.0696**	-0.0603*	-1.308*	-1.315*	-1.631	2.786
	(0.081)	(0.083)	(0.027)	(0.028)	(0.595)	(0.637)	(2.588)	(2.972)
HH member	-0.059	-0.056	-0.005	-0.009	-0.407	-0.450	-0.951	-1.459
	(0.032)	(0.036)	(0.009)	(0.010)	(0.232)	(0.271)	(0.872)	(0.962)
Education	-0.0469*	-0.0595*	-0.0175*	-0.0188*	-0.490**	-0.587**	1.187	0.761
	(0.022)	(0.023)	(0.007)	(0.007)	(0.162)	(0.171)	(0.702)	(0.744)
Training	-0.162	-0.172	0.003	0.034	-0.924	-0.676	6.090	7.588
	(0.158)	(0.165)	(0.049)	(0.050)	(1.142)	(1.185)	(4.744)	(5.069)
Motivation	-0.221*	-0.237*	0.009	0.026	(1.304)	(1.261)	6.403*	5.921
	(0.104)	(0.116)	(0.033)	(0.036)	(0.771)	(0.890)	(3.097)	(3.487)
Past job	0.675**	0.563*	0.141	0.123	5.491**	4.775**	-7.721	-8.827
	(0.238)	(0.261)	(0.072)	(0.071)	(1.693)	(1.817)	(7.656)	(7.844)
Second job	-1.521**	-1.451**	-0.306**	-0.388**	-12.34**	-12.84**	-9.305	-12.600
	(0.206)	(0.263)	(0.070)	(0.085)	(1.462)	(1.857)	(5.607)	(6.590)
Score_raven	0.057	0.071	0.0456**	0.0571**	0.790*	1.012*	1.321	2.249
	(0.053)	(0.059)	(0.016)	(0.018)	(0.387)	(0.462)	(1.590)	(1.817)
Score_numeracy	-0.009	-0.011	-0.012	-0.006	-0.151	-0.119	0.240	0.421
	(0.036)	(0.042)	(0.011)	(0.012)	(0.261)	(0.312)	(1.096)	(1.269)
Score_financial	0.064	0.018	-0.026	-0.020	0.125	-0.087	1.498	0.936
	(0.046)	(0.053)	(0.014)	(0.015)	(0.328)	(0.396)	(1.409)	(1.581)
Risk preference	-1.389	-1.915*	-0.256	-0.153	-11.25*	-13.17*	0.557	-3.766
	(0.741)	(0.825)	(0.222)	(0.229)	(5.436)	(6.021)	(21.870)	(23.450)
Impatience	0.089	0.074	-0.123	-0.127	-0.260	-0.175	1.925	10.430
	(0.314)	(0.348)	(0.100)	(0.108)	(2.261)	(2.595)	(9.365)	(10.010)
CCEI_risk	-0.060	0.123	0.014	-0.007	-1.136	-0.533	21.77*	21.760
	(0.388)	(0.426)	(0.109)	(0.119)	(2.807)	(2.989)	(10.560)	(12.140)
CCEI_time	-0.350	-0.265	-0.017	0.070	-2.434	-1.026	-15.490	-11.600
	(0.461)	(0.479)	(0.138)	(0.147)	(3.303)	(3.286)	(13.690)	(15.280)
Observation	2,465	2,465	2,465	2,465	2,465	2,465	2,465	2,465
TODA fixed effect	No	Yes	No	Yes	No	Yes	No	Yes

continued on next page

Table A1 continued

Panel B	Net salary per day		Driver income per month		Spouse income per month		Household income per month	
	(1)	(2)	(3)	(4)	(5)	(6)	(7)	(8)
Fintech	170.62**	107.09**	5,808.6**	3,855.9**	3,284.5**	3,364.2**	10,404.6**	15,307.1
	(17.74)	(40.43)	(665.7)	(1,382.0)	(737.7)	(1,120.4)	(2,691.5)	(10,829.8)
Male	12.14	28.15	-537.1	-198.5	-2614.1	-1071.5	-2887.3	-508.0
	(41.04)	(41.00)	(1,428.0)	(1,394.8)	(1,353.1)	(1,581.3)	(3,770.2)	(3,486.6)
Married	27.65*	17.480	1172.3**	1028.2**	4131.5**	4083.8**	(1,190.9)	-2045.1*
	(11.44)	(12.81)	(333.5)	(391.1)	(227.0)	(269.8)	(1,064.6)	(844.7)
Age	4.39	4.30	172.6	157.6	467.8**	469.8**	-715.4	-710.7
	-2.56	-2.64	(99.6)	(109.0)	(90.8)	(110.8)	(514.1)	(616.2)
Age2	-0.077**	-0.075**	-2.380*	-2.178	-5.306**	-5.481**	9.325	9.010
	(0.028)	(0.029)	(1.128)	(1.209)	(0.958)	(1.165)	(5.451)	(6.587)
Exp	-1.86	-2.08	-74.70	-78.81	-173.0**	-163.9*	-71.47	-34.02
	(1.33)	(1.40)	(48.92)	(52.00)	(59.03)	(66.18)	(130.00)	(160.90)
Exp2	0.048	0.062	1.983	2.324	3.904**	4.046**	0.726	0.525
	(0.034)	(0.035)	(1.189)	(1.200)	(1.345)	(1.454)	(3.417)	(4.133)
Same province	-20.16*	-14.04	-562.3	-460.2	238.1	346.1	-1665.3*	-1093.7
	(9.36)	(11.38)	(334.0)	(381.1)	(329.9)	(434.8)	(819.5)	(996.4)
Health	-13.88*	-12.20*	-1030.5**	-943.7**	-335.2	-298.50	-1387.6**	-1321.2
	(5.96)	(6.19)	(217.3)	(226.7)	(186.9)	(251.6)	(508.3)	(727.1)
HH member	-2.132	-1.011	8.62	26.40	7.12	94.30	2248.3**	2458.0**
	(2.085)	(1.980)	(73.25)	(79.85)	(76.30)	(90.63)	(292.10)	(258.20)
Education	5.470**	5.757**	229.3**	238.2**	262.9**	281.4**	813.3**	786.3**
	(1.607)	(1.669)	(66.52)	(63.70)	(67.97)	(73.27)	(146.20)	(174.70)
Training	5.260	-2.731	13.18	-7.77	-87.62	-254.90	476.40	-127.10
	(11.410)	(10.800)	(400.10)	(358.00)	(397.40)	(467.00)	(902.00)	(915.40)
Motivation	-3.318	-7.319	335.9	259.7	519.6	610.9*	1869.9*	1761.2*
	(7.938)	(8.157)	(285.7)	(330.2)	(283.6)	(304.6)	(806.9)	(849.2)
Past job	28.89	30.80	460.5	532.2	971.6*	884.7	-610.7	-1108.9
	(17.00)	(20.42)	(582.6)	(701.9)	(480.3)	(574.0)	(4,057.8)	(4,885.7)
Second job	-40.99**	-20.49	4289.1**	4547.0**	-728.30	-699.60	4037.0**	4876.4**
	(12.83)	(13.80)	(574.6)	(641.0)	(384.8)	(449.7)	(1,086.2)	(1,260.9)
Score_raven	6.155	1.075	353.3*	296.5	-68.4	-54.2	400.1	214.2
	(3.757)	(3.711)	(157.2)	(160.9)	(133.9)	(159.5)	(327.2)	(378.3)
Score_numeracy	-4.435	-3.860	-139.50	-136.70	90.98	68.07	-174.30	-33.58
	(2.470)	(2.682)	(88.44)	(109.50)	(84.94)	(95.13)	(188.70)	(233.20)
Score_financial	3.757	1.534	207.0	241.8	8.623	57.72	47.73	247.7
	(3.392)	(3.380)	(117.2)	(127.1)	(110.2)	(131.5)	(269.2)	(268.9)
Risk preference	33.71	27.69	1616.7	2434.4	2605.1	2440.5	5625.4	6477.2
	(55.26)	(63.20)	(1,817.9)	(2,069.0)	(1,874.7)	(2,350.6)	(3,796.6)	(5,416.0)
Impatience	-17.54	-10.35	355.1	584.0	-548.8	-889.1	652.6	403.1
	(21.40)	(23.61)	(988.3)	(1,027.8)	(907.8)	(1,054.7)	(1,844.8)	(1,988.1)
CCEI_risk	-4.98	-10.62	498.00	316.80	56.33	86.81	2097.80	1944.80
	(28.07)	(30.15)	(877.90)	(994.70)	(811.00)	(869.40)	(2,264.40)	(2,592.60)
CCEI_time	-14.51	-8.43	787.10	872.00	-409.50	181.10	-1078.20	-1509.80
	(32.91)	(32.53)	(1,065.20)	(1,087.50)	(1,065.90)	(1,317.80)	(2,698.60)	(2,717.80)
Observation	2,474	2,474	2,474	2,474	2,474	2,474	2,474	2,474
TODA fixed effect	No	Yes	No	Yes	No	Yes	No	Yes

Table A1 continued

Panel C	Loan tenure in month		Total loan amount		Payment amount per week		Payment amount per month	
	(1)	(2)	(3)	(4)	(5)	(6)	(7)	(8)
Fintech	14.93**	11.06**	173695.8**	142425.6**	204.9*	191.2*	2852.0**	2031.6**
	(0.775)	(1.856)	(6,857.2)	(22,744.9)	(79.1)	(90.2)	(104.7)	(369.8)
Male	-0.708	-1.616	-1898.1	-6333.3	-118.4	35.62	-33.87	-141.6
	(2.552)	(3.288)	(12,228.0)	(13,583.6)	(102.0)	(75.14)	(210.10)	(254.8)
Married	0.197	0.435	-2410.8	-9374.8	-87.11	-33.76	-59.21	-208.6
	(0.866)	(0.925)	(7,848.8)	(9,259.5)	(96.58)	(62.18)	(160.50)	(234.3)
Age	0.294	0.312	-173.1	-1160.1	5.41	-3.60	-31.51	-43.04
	(0.206)	(0.221)	(1,512.4)	(1,772.4)	(12.33)	(12.94)	(28.02)	(42.14)
Age2	-0.004	-0.004	-5.633	7.411	-0.056	0.080	0.267	0.428
	(0.0023)	(0.0024)	(16.230)	(19.340)	(0.149)	(0.156)	(0.312)	(0.472)
Exp	-0.177	-0.090	-410.50	449.30	-2.92	-2.41	33.49*	42.09
	(0.091)	(0.127)	(649.10)	(929.90)	(5.41)	(7.54)	(13.02)	(22.03)
Exp2	0.004	0.003	6.169	-11.650	0.027	0.069	-0.801*	-0.977*
	(0.002)	(0.003)	(16.010)	(21.300)	(0.171)	(0.200)	(0.340)	(0.477)
Same province	-2.376**	-0.375	-16572.8**	246.2	-116.6**	31.84	-224.7*	-73.27
	(0.652)	(0.883)	(4,664.4)	(5,629.0)	(44.82)	(54.78)	(89.43)	(101.10)
Health	0.737	0.304	3474.2	1434.3	4.23	10.53	62.05	48.25
	(0.433)	(0.450)	(3,014.6)	(3,161.4)	(25.84)	(23.67)	(55.82)	(68.24)
HH member	0.019	-0.158	-256.7	-196.9	4.106	11.750	-2.517	30.30
	(0.155)	(0.196)	(1,104.7)	(1,014.3)	(8.397)	(8.646)	(21.470)	(25.15)
Education	0.179	0.224	1216.9	1487.3	0.639	1.719	20.24	7.518
	(0.126)	(0.120)	(822.4)	(858.7)	(5.802)	(6.620)	(17.34)	(24.990)
Training	-0.329	-0.818	-4075.9	-10185.9	18.88	19.15	30.68	11.28
	(0.765)	(0.922)	(5,526.9)	(6,756.3)	(43.82)	(60.42)	(102.40)	(133.90)
Motivation	-0.659	-0.462	-6144.7	-3026.5	56.79	19.27	-35.53	-29.24
	(0.536)	(0.585)	(4,932.3)	(5,117.9)	(52.44)	(38.83)	(117.60)	(144.40)
Past job	1.365	1.755	19782.6*	15514.0	33.60	-31.28	187.70	88.11
	(1.194)	(1.474)	(9,057.3)	(11,980.5)	(97.57)	(150.20)	(209.30)	(275.10)
Second job	-1.379	-1.286	-6721.8	-3728.3	20.30	66.46	-51.97	5.896
	(0.843)	(1.077)	(7,257.8)	(9,725.9)	(47.94)	(46.26)	(113.80)	(159.30)
Score_raven	-0.553*	-0.706*	31.83	-278.5	2.807	14.57	40.65	32.30
	(0.274)	(0.319)	(2,252.2)	(2,383.1)	(17.55)	(14.64)	(37.13)	(41.97)
Score_numeracy	0.132	0.034	-1501.2	-723.6	-4.116	-8.125	-55.51	-13.91
	(0.181)	(0.204)	(1,325.2)	(1,452.1)	(10.47)	(13.74)	(28.97)	(33.89)
Score_financial	-0.417	-0.190	-2515.3	-690.5	13.85	12.14	35.33	67.74
	(0.245)	(0.269)	(1,778.1)	(2,296.2)	(15.83)	(14.33)	(38.28)	(53.79)
Risk preference	1.252	-6.480	25510.8	-14706.2	725.7**	448.2	1239.0*	1284.8
	(3.843)	(4.569)	(26,431.5)	(32,604.3)	(247.5)	(273.2)	(544.4)	(817.5)
Impatience	1.393	0.534	15754.0	20439.9	313.7*	137.5	481.5	550.4
	(1.605)	(1.881)	(12,597.5)	(14,588.0)	(122.7)	(111.9)	(284.9)	(439.6)
CCEI_risk	0.228	-0.733	21711.7	23487.1	99.03	96.41	353.7	466.5
	(2.085)	(2.304)	(14,720.4)	(16,175.0)	(100.80)	(79.65)	(252.2)	(319.9)
CCEI_time	0.381	1.672	-18745.0	-22703.8	-91.41	-49.26	7.383	-223.2
	(2.312)	(2.675)	(18,122.8)	(17,766.4)	(118.0)	(141.0)	(302.3)	(359.2)
Observation	1,080	1,080	1,079	1,079	324	324	978	978
TODA fixed effect	No	Yes	No	Yes	No	Yes	No	Yes

continued on next page

Table A1 continued

Panel D	Have a budget		Have a financial goal		Prepared a plan		Increased credit card	
	(1)	(2)	(3)	(4)	(5)	(6)	(7)	(8)
Fintech	0.0544*	0.0652	0.136**	0.0246	-0.00563	-0.114	0.0195	0.0669
	(0.0270)	(0.0615)	(0.0316)	(0.0481)	(0.0386)	(0.0827)	(0.0173)	(0.0731)
Male	0.107	0.113	0.0491	0.0856	-0.0504	-0.106	0.0211*	0.00349
	(0.0796)	(0.0813)	(0.0850)	(0.1020)	(0.1020)	(0.1240)	(0.0102)	(0.0187)
Married	0.0931**	0.0823*	0.0377	0.0141	0.0572	0.0514	0.0247*	0.0253
	(0.0259)	(0.0322)	(0.0267)	(0.0298)	(0.0375)	(0.0516)	(0.0107)	(0.0141)
Age	-0.00465	-0.00225	-0.00871	-0.0078	-0.00722	-0.00283	-0.00102	0.00177
	(0.00551)	(0.00607)	(0.00599)	(0.00664)	(0.00816)	(0.01070)	(0.00311)	(0.00367)
Age2	0.00006	0.00003	0.00007	0.00005	0.00007	0.00002	0.000009	-0.00002
	(0.00006)	(0.00007)	(0.00007)	(0.00007)	(0.00009)	(0.00010)	(0.00003)	(0.00004)
Exp	-0.0001	-0.0005	-0.0008	0.0008	0.004	0.0005	0.003	0.0006
	(0.003)	(0.003)	(0.003)	(0.003)	(0.004)	(0.007)	(0.001)	(0.002)
Exp2	-0.000007	0.00002	-0.000005	-0.000007	-0.0002	-0.0001	-0.00007*	-0.00001
	(0.00007)	(0.00008)	(0.00008)	(0.00009)	(0.00010)	(0.00020)	(0.00003)	(0.00004)
Same province	-0.00817	0.00448	0.0157	0.0474*	-0.0168	-0.00646	-0.0069	-0.000929
	(0.0190)	(0.0222)	(0.0207)	(0.0235)	(0.0279)	(0.0357)	(0.0107)	(0.0133)
Health	-0.0137	-0.00591	-0.00893	-0.00259	-0.0139	0.000886	0.0074	0.00956
	(0.0121)	(0.0150)	(0.0131)	(0.0149)	(0.0174)	(0.0206)	(0.0083)	(0.0115)
HH member	0.000927	0.00176	-0.00591	-0.00405	-0.00023	-0.00049	-0.00660**	-0.00449
	(0.00450)	(0.00505)	(0.00480)	(0.00485)	(0.00663)	(0.00810)	(0.00239)	(0.00325)
Education	0.0149**	0.0150**	0.0168**	0.0157**	0.0119*	0.0171**	0.00148	0.00244
	(0.00328)	(0.00367)	(0.00361)	(0.00394)	(0.00468)	(0.00656)	(0.00166)	(0.00203)
Training	0.0586**	0.0525*	0.0287	0.026	-0.0237	-0.0644	0.00354	-0.0101
	(0.0217)	(0.0238)	(0.0254)	(0.0253)	(0.0323)	(0.0389)	(0.0124)	(0.0155)
Motivation	-0.0125	-0.00486	-0.0126	-0.0128	-0.0086	-0.00326	-0.00485	-0.0228*
	(0.0157)	(0.0178)	(0.0169)	(0.0190)	(0.0221)	(0.0285)	(0.0072)	(0.0105)
Past job	-0.0123	-0.00954	-0.00929	-0.0111	-0.0226	-0.0383	-0.0268	-0.0256
	(0.0352)	(0.0380)	(0.0384)	(0.0422)	(0.0485)	(0.0644)	(0.0256)	(0.0292)
Second job	0.0389	0.0292	0.0504	0.0323	-0.0419	-0.0271	-0.0108	0.00808
	(0.0244)	(0.0278)	(0.0283)	(0.0293)	(0.0356)	(0.0460)	(0.0129)	(0.0162)
Score_raven	0.0151	0.00804	0.0435**	0.0345**	-0.00536	-0.00301	0.0115*	0.0131
	(0.0081)	(0.0097)	(0.0087)	(0.0097)	(0.0118)	(0.0149)	(0.0057)	(0.0080)
Score_numeracy	-0.00476	-0.00369	0.00562	0.00567	-0.00362	-0.00833	-0.00455	-0.00274
	(0.00538)	(0.00651)	(0.00585)	(0.00649)	(0.00752)	(0.01040)	(0.00279)	(0.00410)
Score_financial	0.00777	0.00834	0.0188*	0.0218*	-0.0122	-0.0146	-0.00897*	-0.0102
	(0.00722)	(0.00872)	(0.00764)	(0.00938)	(0.01050)	(0.01430)	(0.00422)	(0.00605)
Risk preference	0.0282	0.0772	0.0976	0.0617	-0.0619	-0.00608	0.00647	-0.0485
	(0.115)	(0.131)	(0.117)	(0.140)	(0.142)	(0.199)	(0.059)	(0.074)
Impatience	-0.0552	-0.0473	-0.0411	-0.0366	-0.0928	-0.0900	-0.0137	-0.0375
	(0.0452)	(0.0506)	(0.0501)	(0.0609)	(0.0633)	(0.0781)	(0.0251)	(0.0308)
CCEI_risk	0.0700	0.0531	0.0176	0.0565	0.0215	-0.0431	0.0399	0.0212
	(0.0564)	(0.0645)	(0.0608)	(0.0638)	(0.0785)	(0.0899)	(0.0254)	(0.0364)
CCEI_time	-0.143*	-0.12	0.103	0.129	-0.0731	0.0419	-0.0323	-0.0253
	(0.0667)	(0.0759)	(0.0752)	(0.0802)	(0.0994)	(0.1180)	(0.0404)	(0.0581)
Observation	2,473	2,473	2,474	2,474	1,103	1,103	1,103	1,103
TODA fixed effect	No	Yes	No	Yes	No	Yes	No	Yes

continued on next page

Table A1 continued

Panel E	Saved/invested money		Looked for additional work		Identified a source of credit		Cut back on spending	
	(1)	(2)	(3)	(4)	(5)	(6)	(7)	(8)
Fintech	-0.0160	0.1830	-0.0219	-0.0439	-0.0810**	-0.0216	-0.0829*	-0.1260
	(0.0395)	(0.1240)	(0.0417)	(0.1420)	(0.0225)	(0.0546)	(0.0391)	(0.1020)
Male	0.1880	0.2040	0.0189	-0.0300	0.0275	0.0656	0.1310	-0.0232
	(0.1190)	(0.1380)	(0.1190)	(0.1260)	(0.0641)	(0.0975)	(0.1190)	(0.1730)
Married	-0.0108	-0.0080	0.0885*	0.0767	0.0598**	0.0640*	0.0479	0.0527
	(0.0338)	(0.0472)	(0.0380)	(0.0546)	(0.0207)	(0.0273)	(0.0356)	(0.0474)
Age	-0.0041	-0.0155	0.0184*	0.0173	0.0016	0.0067	-0.0019	-0.0144
	(0.0083)	(0.0112)	(0.0082)	(0.0116)	(0.0062)	(0.0083)	(0.0078)	(0.0093)
Age2	0.00005	0.0002	-0.0003**	-0.0002	-0.00001	-0.00008	0.00001	0.0002
	(0.0001)	(0.0001)	(0.00009)	(0.0001)	(0.00007)	(0.00009)	(0.00009)	(0.0001)
Exp	-0.00283	0.00215	-0.0101*	-0.0120*	-0.00195	-0.00189	-0.00956*	-0.00456
	(0.00407)	(0.00542)	(0.00432)	(0.00587)	(0.00285)	(0.00421)	(0.00373)	(0.00481)
Exp2	0.00009	-0.00001	0.0002*	0.0003	0.00004	0.00008	0.0003**	0.0002
	(0.0001)	(0.0001)	(0.0001)	(0.0002)	(0.0001)	(0.0001)	(0.0001)	(0.0001)
Same province	-0.0106	-0.0132	-0.00394	-0.00155	0.0209	0.00932	-0.0121	0.00171
	(0.0272)	(0.0361)	(0.0294)	(0.0464)	(0.0189)	(0.0244)	(0.0263)	(0.0360)
Health	-0.0516**	-0.0515*	0.0135	-0.011	0.0045	0.00593	-0.0283	-0.0247
	(0.0181)	(0.0227)	(0.0193)	(0.0271)	(0.0118)	(0.0139)	(0.0173)	(0.0248)
HH member	-0.0137*	-0.0178*	0.00751	0.0119	-0.00488	-0.00495	-0.00244	-0.00443
	(0.0063)	(0.0086)	(0.00673)	(0.00845)	(0.00398)	(0.00558)	(0.00650)	(0.00789)
Education	0.0187**	0.0196**	0.00786	0.0104	-0.0058	-0.00466	-0.00313	0.00114
	(0.00467)	(0.00535)	(0.00524)	(0.00628)	(0.00317)	(0.00433)	(0.00465)	(0.00665)
Training	-0.0247	-0.0175	0.0453	0.0334	-0.0266	-0.0319	0.0519	0.0329
	(0.0316)	(0.0408)	(0.0346)	(0.0470)	(0.0197)	(0.0266)	(0.0289)	(0.0372)
Motivation	-0.0198	-0.0101	0.00307	-0.00926	0.0183	0.00714	-0.00775	0.00583
	(0.0228)	(0.0276)	(0.0245)	(0.0288)	(0.0150)	(0.0221)	(0.0215)	(0.0285)
Past job	0.0452	0.00835	-0.0357	0.0273	0.0465	0.0446	-0.0203	-0.037
	(0.0542)	(0.0700)	(0.0567)	(0.0727)	(0.0278)	(0.0450)	(0.0470)	(0.0625)
Second job	-0.0231	-0.00345	0.313**	0.299**	0.0272	0.0117	-0.0862*	-0.0583
	(0.0350)	(0.0512)	(0.0387)	(0.0556)	(0.0249)	(0.0283)	(0.0357)	(0.0466)
Score_raven	-0.00366	-0.00618	-0.00849	-0.0061	0.00935	0.0102	-0.0000632	-0.0114
	(0.0115)	(0.0146)	(0.0125)	(0.0164)	(0.0073)	(0.0090)	(0.0111)	(0.0146)
Score_numeracy	-0.0141	-0.0219*	0.0172*	0.0111	-0.00924	-0.00333	0.000027	-0.0049
	(0.0081)	(0.00999)	(0.0086)	(0.0107)	(0.00518)	(0.00721)	(0.00731)	(0.0086)
Score_financial	-0.0125	-0.00462	-0.00237	-0.000585	-0.0193**	-0.0145	0.0163	0.0162
	(0.00996)	(0.01410)	(0.01090)	(0.01440)	(0.00745)	(0.0094)	(0.0098)	(0.0128)
Risk preference	0.1080	0.2250	0.2660	0.0699	0.0091	-0.0879	-0.0704	0.1280
	(0.1650)	(0.2020)	(0.1800)	(0.2510)	(0.0935)	(0.1170)	(0.1440)	(0.1960)
Impatience	0.0019	-0.0630	-0.0011	-0.0398	0.0074	-0.0075	0.0370	0.0353
	(0.0635)	(0.0900)	(0.0716)	(0.0838)	(0.0408)	(0.0506)	(0.0606)	(0.0702)
CCEI_risk	0.1260	0.0665	-0.0681	-0.0019	-0.0050	-0.0122	0.0635	0.0221
	(0.0870)	(0.1010)	(0.0898)	(0.1110)	(0.0523)	(0.0727)	(0.0769)	(0.0960)
CCEI_time	-0.0590	-0.0161	-0.0649	-0.1500	0.0222	-0.0149	-0.0238	-0.0457
	(0.1000)	(0.1230)	(0.1130)	(0.1590)	(0.0632)	(0.0918)	(0.0919)	(0.1230)
Observation	1,103	1,103	1,103	1,103	1,103	1,103	1,103	1,103
TODA fixed effect	No	Yes	No	Yes	No	Yes	No	Yes

continued on next page

Table A1 continued

Panel F	Bank account ownership		Debit card ownership		Credit card ownership		Online/mobile banking	
	(1)	(2)	(3)	(4)	(5)	(6)	(7)	(8)
Fintech	0.0953**	-0.0221	0.0897**	0.0302	-0.00009	0.0022	0.0122	0.0297
	(0.0283)	(0.0772)	(0.0244)	(0.0594)	(0.0070)	(0.0170)	(0.0097)	(0.0227)
Male	0.0043	-0.0305	0.0211	-0.0002	0.0124**	0.0101	-0.0030	-0.0007
	(0.0674)	(0.0662)	(0.0489)	(0.0553)	(0.0039)	(0.0062)	(0.0282)	(0.0325)
Married	0.0248	0.0271	0.0218	0.0236	0.0051	0.0091	0.0020	0.0030
	(0.0218)	(0.0252)	(0.0179)	(0.0193)	(0.0057)	(0.0060)	(0.0080)	(0.0094)
Age	-0.0188**	-0.0167**	-0.0144**	-0.0148**	0.0012	0.0011	-0.0021	-0.0023
	(0.0052)	(0.0054)	(0.0044)	(0.0045)	(0.0013)	(0.0013)	(0.0016)	(0.0017)
Age2	0.0003**	0.0002**	0.0002**	0.0002**	-0.00001	-0.00001	0.00001	0.00001
	(0.00006)	(0.00006)	(0.00005)	(0.00005)	(0.00001)	(0.00001)	(0.00002)	(0.00002)
Exp	0.00092	0.00260	0.00068	0.00092	-0.00104	-0.00115	-0.00060	-0.00065
	(0.00262)	(0.00306)	(0.00220)	(0.00257)	(0.00066)	(0.00076)	(0.00081)	(0.00102)
Exp2	-0.00006	-0.0001	-0.00004	-0.00008	0.00002	0.00002	0.00001	0.00001
	(0.00007)	(0.00007)	(0.00006)	(0.00006)	(0.00002)	(0.00002)	(0.00002)	(0.00002)
Same province	-0.0312	-0.0256	-0.0227	-0.0216	-0.0006	-0.0006	0.0129*	0.0131*
	(0.0171)	(0.0213)	(0.0139)	(0.0158)	(0.0044)	(0.0048)	(0.0055)	(0.0060)
Health	-0.00828	-0.0153	-0.00567	-0.0192*	0.0000572	0.000834	0.000434	0.00104
	(0.0113)	(0.0113)	(0.0094)	(0.0087)	(0.0030)	(0.0033)	(0.0039)	(0.0043)
HH member	0.00431	0.0034	-0.00276	-0.00311	-0.00208*	-0.00196*	-0.00122	-0.000417
	(0.00412)	(0.00461)	(0.00327)	(0.00396)	(0.00096)	(0.00098)	(0.00130)	(0.00140)
Education	0.0218**	0.0191**	0.0165**	0.0147**	0.00154	0.00141	0.00298**	0.00306*
	(0.00314)	(0.00333)	(0.00268)	(0.00296)	(0.00083)	(0.00074)	(0.00097)	(0.00121)
Training	-0.00421	-0.00335	-0.00846	-0.00879	0.0131*	0.00905	0.00791	0.00579
	(0.02190)	(0.02340)	(0.01830)	(0.01980)	(0.00661)	(0.00674)	(0.00792)	(0.00921)
Motivation	-0.0129	-0.011	-0.0118	-0.0081	0.00345	0.0048	0.00305	0.00188
	(0.0147)	(0.0151)	(0.0118)	(0.0126)	(0.0041)	(0.0047)	(0.0048)	(0.0057)
Past job	0.0723*	0.0839*	0.0552**	0.0573*	-0.00428	-0.00536	-0.00937	-0.00816
	(0.0285)	(0.0336)	(0.0209)	(0.0237)	(0.0088)	(0.0099)	(0.0125)	(0.0136)
Second job	0.0800**	0.0676*	0.0559*	0.0475	0.0003	0.0056	0.0117	0.0140
	(0.0257)	(0.0301)	(0.0218)	(0.0251)	(0.0064)	(0.0090)	(0.0097)	(0.0110)
Score_raven	0.0066	0.0131	0.0131*	0.0176**	0.0039	0.0041	0.0019	0.0012
	(0.0073)	(0.0080)	(0.0060)	(0.0065)	(0.0020)	(0.0022)	(0.0025)	(0.0031)
Score_numeracy	0.0105*	0.0107	0.0051	0.0044	0.0013	0.0010	0.0013	0.0011
	(0.0049)	(0.0055)	(0.0039)	(0.0043)	(0.0011)	(0.0013)	(0.0015)	(0.0015)
Score_financial	0.0100	0.0119	0.0056	0.0095	0.0012	0.0003	0.0011	-0.0003
	(0.0063)	(0.0074)	(0.0051)	(0.0057)	(0.0014)	(0.0013)	(0.0018)	(0.0021)
Risk preference	0.1400	0.1620	0.229**	0.233**	0.0381	0.0197	0.0137	0.0248
	(0.1010)	(0.1020)	(0.0837)	(0.0865)	(0.0247)	(0.0238)	(0.0285)	(0.0312)
Impatience	0.0306	0.0467	0.0093	0.0204	-0.0018	-0.0023	-0.0027	-0.0015
	(0.0420)	(0.0448)	(0.0340)	(0.0372)	(0.0122)	(0.0133)	(0.0123)	(0.0118)
CCEI_risk	0.0329	0.0037	-0.0089	-0.0025	0.0036	0.0092	0.0151	0.0221
	(0.0493)	(0.0579)	(0.0396)	(0.0452)	(0.0099)	(0.0114)	(0.0150)	(0.0202)
CCEI_time	-0.0200	0.0177	0.0648	0.0671	-0.0142	-0.0116	-0.0279	-0.0324
	(0.0606)	(0.0718)	(0.0470)	(0.0554)	(0.0176)	(0.0199)	(0.0227)	(0.0276)
Observation	2,474	2,474	2,474	2,474	2,474	2,474	2,474	2,474
TODA fixed effect	No	Yes	No	Yes	No	Yes	No	Yes

continued on next page

Table A1 continued

Panel G	Saved for some reason		Saved for old age		Saved for business	
	(1)	(2)	(3)	(4)	(5)	(6)
Fintech	0.0772*	-0.0441	0.0478	0.0495	0.0739**	0.0432
	(0.0318)	(0.0734)	(0.0265)	(0.0567)	(0.0231)	(0.0634)
Male	0.0841	0.1420	0.0451	0.0766	-0.0354	0.0008
	(0.0767)	(0.0882)	(0.0537)	(0.0610)	(0.0542)	(0.0668)
Married	0.0196	-0.0026	0.0402*	0.0299	0.0277	0.0163
	(0.0270)	(0.0320)	(0.0204)	(0.0229)	(0.0154)	(0.0179)
Age	-0.0030	-0.0061	0.0055	0.0059	-0.0012	-0.0006
	(0.0061)	(0.0068)	(0.0045)	(0.0053)	(0.0035)	(0.0036)
Age2	0.00002	0.00005	-0.00004	-0.00004	0.000005	-0.0000003
	(0.00007)	(0.00007)	(0.00005)	(0.00006)	(0.00004)	(0.00004)
Exp	-0.0056	-0.0030	-0.0007	-0.0004	-0.0018	0.0011
	(0.0031)	(0.0032)	(0.0025)	(0.0028)	(0.0018)	(0.0021)
Exp2	0.00010	0.00007	-0.00001	-0.00003	0.00002	-0.00004
	(0.00008)	(0.00008)	(0.00006)	(0.00007)	(0.00004)	(0.00005)
Same province	-0.0067	0.0066	-0.0254	-0.0183	-0.0424**	-0.0319*
	(0.0210)	(0.0242)	(0.0167)	(0.0208)	(0.0125)	(0.0146)
Health	-0.0218	-0.0114	-0.0221*	-0.0219	-0.0116	-0.0127
	(0.0133)	(0.0151)	(0.0102)	(0.0112)	(0.0080)	(0.0086)
HH member	-0.0137**	-0.0108	-0.0047	-0.0047	-0.00557*	-0.0044
	(0.0048)	(0.0056)	(0.0038)	(0.0045)	(0.0028)	(0.0033)
Education	0.0172**	0.0143**	0.0206**	0.0179**	0.0056*	0.0055*
	(0.0036)	(0.0042)	(0.0029)	(0.0035)	(0.0023)	(0.0026)
Training	0.0709**	0.0734*	0.0598**	0.0574*	-0.0004	0.0009
	(0.0257)	(0.0294)	(0.0218)	(0.0236)	(0.0158)	(0.0195)
Motivation	-0.0210	-0.0197	0.0127	0.0120	-0.0103	-0.0147
	(0.0172)	(0.0197)	(0.0131)	(0.0145)	(0.0108)	(0.0119)
Past job	0.0620	0.0767	0.0158	0.0235	0.0393*	0.0370
	(0.0384)	(0.0428)	(0.0297)	(0.0324)	(0.0189)	(0.0214)
Second job	0.0385	0.0322	0.0417	0.0338	0.0193	0.0326
	(0.0287)	(0.0291)	(0.0239)	(0.0244)	(0.0187)	(0.0235)
Score_raven	0.0062	0.0066	-0.0025	-0.0009	0.0015	0.0014
	(0.0089)	(0.0095)	(0.0067)	(0.0083)	(0.0056)	(0.0064)
Score_numeracy	-0.0008	0.0024	-0.0072	-0.0019	-0.0012	-0.0001
	(0.0059)	(0.0066)	(0.0047)	(0.0050)	(0.0035)	(0.0044)
Score_financial	-0.0062	-0.0082	0.0066	0.0031	0.0017	0.0043
	(0.0077)	(0.0097)	(0.0061)	(0.0076)	(0.0045)	(0.0053)
Risk preference	0.1100	0.0902	-0.0022	-0.0018	0.0292	0.0186
	(0.1210)	(0.1480)	(0.0969)	(0.1180)	(0.0742)	(0.0829)
Impatience	0.0327	-0.0149	0.0085	-0.0120	0.0001	-0.0176
	(0.0502)	(0.0539)	(0.0403)	(0.0428)	(0.0320)	(0.0406)
CCEI_risk	0.0921	0.1090	0.0597	0.0694	0.0176	0.0065
	(0.0604)	(0.0645)	(0.0474)	(0.0513)	(0.0351)	(0.0386)
CCEI_time	-0.1170	-0.1600	-0.0571	-0.0957	-0.0108	-0.0200
	(0.0756)	(0.0833)	(0.0594)	(0.0658)	(0.0434)	(0.0473)
Observation	2,474	2,474	2,474	2,474	2,474	2,474
TODA fixed effect	No	Yes	No	Yes	No	Yes

continued on next page

Table A1 continued

Panel H	Have cash/ savings at home		Have savings at financial institution		Have savings through family members		Have savingsg at informal savings group	
	(1)	(2)	(3)	(4)	(5)	(6)	(7)	(8)
Fintech	0.0393	-0.0614	0.0780**	0.0575	0.0197	-0.0045	0.0489*	0.0391
	(0.0305)	(0.0716)	(0.0203)	(0.0366)	(0.0173)	(0.0449)	(0.0225)	(0.0435)
Male	0.0879	0.1250	-0.0078	0.0351	0.0492	0.0572	-0.0060	-0.0280
	(0.0731)	(0.0901)	(0.0442)	(0.0449)	(0.0288)	(0.0298)	(0.0533)	(0.0747)
Married	0.0276	0.0179	0.0097	0.0144	-0.0263	-0.0298	0.0199	0.0129
	(0.0257)	(0.0314)	(0.0128)	(0.0155)	(0.0154)	(0.0189)	(0.0152)	(0.0173)
Age	-0.0025	-0.0050	-0.0021	-0.0024	-0.00749*	-0.00883*	0.0014	0.0012
	(0.0058)	(0.0064)	(0.0032)	(0.0041)	(0.0033)	(0.0037)	(0.0034)	(0.0037)
Age2	0.00001	0.00004	0.00003	0.00003	0.00007*	0.00008*	-0.00002	-0.00001
	(0.00006)	(0.00007)	(0.00004)	(0.00005)	(0.00003)	(0.00004)	(0.00004)	(0.00004)
Exp	-0.00578	-0.00330	-0.00160	-0.00137	-0.00077	0.00180	-0.00217	-0.00189
	(0.00297)	(0.00348)	(0.00158)	(0.00167)	(0.00145)	(0.00174)	(0.00196)	(0.00218)
Exp2	0.00010	0.00007	0.00002	0.00001	0.00003	-0.00002	0.00005	0.00003
	(0.00008)	(0.00009)	(0.00004)	(0.00004)	(0.00004)	(0.00004)	(0.00005)	(0.00005)
Same province	-0.0047	0.0040	0.0017	0.0098	0.0126	0.0220	-0.0159	0.0060
	(0.0199)	(0.0226)	(0.0101)	(0.0121)	(0.0101)	(0.0118)	(0.0131)	(0.0172)
Health	-0.0151	-0.0066	-0.0077	-0.0107	-0.0137*	-0.0113	-0.0138	-0.0178*
	(0.0127)	(0.0146)	(0.0070)	(0.0076)	(0.0058)	(0.0068)	(0.0074)	(0.0077)
HH member	-0.0082	-0.0070	-0.0022	-0.0015	0.0015	0.0026	-0.0001	0.0016
	(0.0046)	(0.0054)	(0.0025)	(0.0030)	(0.0028)	(0.0029)	(0.0029)	(0.0033)
Education	0.0119**	0.0077	0.0110**	0.0101**	0.00473*	0.0045	0.00550*	0.0042
	(0.0035)	(0.0041)	(0.0020)	(0.0022)	(0.0020)	(0.0025)	(0.0023)	(0.0032)
Training	0.0402	0.0445	0.0193	0.0222	0.0192	0.0138	0.0381*	0.0440*
	(0.0246)	(0.0297)	(0.0144)	(0.0158)	(0.0137)	(0.0146)	(0.0172)	(0.0183)
Motivation	-0.0170	-0.0141	-0.0035	-0.0012	0.0002	-0.0005	-0.0143	-0.0135
	(0.0161)	(0.0190)	(0.0085)	(0.0091)	(0.0080)	(0.0100)	(0.0099)	(0.0109)
Past job	0.0546	0.0572	0.0380**	0.0391*	0.0224	0.0175	-0.0026	0.0109
	(0.0350)	(0.0420)	(0.0127)	(0.0155)	(0.0172)	(0.0212)	(0.0236)	(0.0274)
Second job	0.0011	-0.0010	0.0369*	0.0307	0.0196	0.0159	0.0044	0.0124
	(0.0274)	(0.0284)	(0.0171)	(0.0187)	(0.0159)	(0.0181)	(0.0181)	(0.0212)
Score_raven	0.0088	0.0105	0.0037	0.0030	-0.0020	-0.0032	0.0047	0.0037
	(0.0084)	(0.0091)	(0.0045)	(0.0051)	(0.0045)	(0.0050)	(0.0053)	(0.0058)
Score_numeracy	-0.0070	-0.0037	-0.0023	-0.0025	-0.0009	-0.0004	-0.0028	-0.0018
	(0.0056)	(0.0063)	(0.0028)	(0.0031)	(0.0030)	(0.0034)	(0.0034)	(0.0041)
Score_financial	-0.0135	-0.0101	0.00882*	0.0064	-0.0109**	-0.0112*	-0.0018	0.0007
	(0.0073)	(0.0087)	(0.0038)	(0.0044)	(0.0041)	(0.0049)	(0.0046)	(0.0054)
Risk preference	0.0916	0.0977	0.0328	0.0289	-0.0387	-0.0227	0.0362	0.0067
	(0.1160)	(0.1350)	(0.0623)	(0.0742)	(0.0620)	(0.0798)	(0.0747)	(0.0841)
Impatience	-0.0022	-0.0285	0.0188	0.0031	0.0335	0.0280	-0.0117	-0.0269
	(0.0479)	(0.0524)	(0.0247)	(0.0272)	(0.0259)	(0.0304)	(0.0296)	(0.0324)
CCEI_risk	0.0435	0.0598	0.0306	0.0492	0.0101	0.0041	-0.0007	0.0091
	(0.0563)	(0.0648)	(0.0280)	(0.0325)	(0.0302)	(0.0342)	(0.0370)	(0.0436)
CCEI_time	-0.0281	-0.0654	-0.0387	-0.0350	-0.0430	-0.0600	-0.109*	-0.132*
	(0.0723)	(0.0812)	(0.0392)	(0.0460)	(0.0382)	(0.0451)	(0.0488)	(0.0539)
Observation	2,474	2,474	2,474	2,474	2,474	2,474	2,474	2,474
TODA fixed effect	No	Yes	No	Yes	No	Yes	No	Yes

continued on next page

Table A1 continued

Panel I	Savings in cash		Savings at financial institution		Savings through family members		Savings at informal savings group	
	(1)	(2)	(3)	(4)	(5)	(6)	(7)	(8)
Fintech	2993.8	403.4	18274.7*	36248.7	5703.6	-12078.4	3081.3	2238.6
	(1,993.6)	(6,786.8)	(8,943.4)	(39,594.1)	(4,133.7)	(9,635.5)	(3,506.4)	(6,113.9)
Male	1886.5	6310.8	-3088.1	-19654.5	5858.7	0	9281.9	0
	(4,849.1)	(7,013.1)	(16,490.9)	(46,088.8)	(3,891.3)	(.)	(5,139.6)	(.)
Married	665	407	-14791.7	-887.7	1487.1	-1909.5	-2807.9	6655.4
	(1,557.7)	(2,461.7)	(13,583.4)	(33,554.9)	(2,077.1)	(10,197.7)	(4,214.9)	(8,377.6)
Age	-444.1	-690.3	-775.8	2303.7	-28.81	2145.6	676.1	894.7
	(342.5)	(566.1)	(1,431.2)	(8,256.9)	(661.3)	(2,439.5)	(775.1)	(2,177.0)
Age2	4.277	6.470	8.327	-17.78	-0.544	-29.010	-6.509	-9.607
	(3.765)	(6.383)	(15.620)	(84.010)	(8.080)	(29.960)	(9.093)	(24.840)
Exp	203.0	208.3	2959.0*	3713.1	-385.5	-1678.7*	197.0	-97.2
	(176.3)	(313.7)	(1,241.1)	(4,909.2)	(334.2)	(785.0)	(333.4)	(816.4)
Exp2	-5.892	-3.565	-75.00*	-159.0	14.61	64.42*	-6.724	8.813
	(4.603)	(8.268)	(31.32)	(202.7)	(10.42)	(26.62)	(9.692)	(21.970)
Same province	-1787.4	-2945.6	-5927.5	24931.3	-2638.2	8093.1	-4207.1	7536.1
	(1,211.6)	(1,815.2)	(7,919.9)	(29,904.1)	(2,367.4)	(6,723.7)	(2,765.9)	(8,593.1)
Health	-2876.5**	-3884.6**	-2674.7	-1843.3	788	-3956.5	-1203	3461.1
	(693.3)	(1,140.9)	(3,762.9)	(13,475.5)	(1,501.6)	(5,754.6)	(2,176.7)	(6,048.4)
HH member	-59.95	16.12	778.8	-2692.2	-683.6	-316.3	-607.6	-845.4
	(305.5)	(397.7)	(1,950.3)	(5,307.0)	(437.6)	(1,270.7)	(690.0)	(1,361.1)
Education	536.0*	465	414.8	539.7	210.9	775.2	222.8	1032.7
	(227.2)	(331.6)	(1,087.2)	(3,761.6)	(423.9)	(882.1)	(473.5)	(1,157.8)
Training	2127.4	1646.2	5420	-9894.6	-2562.8	8263.3	-182.4	-1715.7
	(1,493.6)	(2,085.8)	(7,927.2)	(26,664.2)	(1,825.1)	(10,838.8)	(2,780.7)	(6,659.9)
Motivation	617.2	1339.7	5109.1	19492.8	-612.8	6047.6	946.0	1714.2
	(1,143.5)	(1,567.0)	(6,885.3)	(19,825.9)	(2,222.4)	(6,567.1)	(2,197.0)	(6,648.0)
Past job	-3210.4	-3533.0	534.4	6450.2	7417.9*	12947.5	-5958.1	-5039.4
	(2,766.9)	(3,873.6)	(10,962.2)	(51,465.3)	(3,413.8)	(15,849.1)	(4,644.6)	(11,746.2)
Second job	773.5	2409.7	-6912.5	-213.0	-2286.1	4061.0	-4866.7	-9985.2
	(1,782.6)	(2,336.4)	(7,084.8)	(28,517.3)	(1,896.6)	(7,473.7)	(2,719.0)	(12,451.4)
Score_raven	-601.4	-963.0	-732.3	-10162.7	277.7	2004.9	277.5	1588.1
	(535.0)	(701.1)	(4,043.9)	(11,221.7)	(912.9)	(2,832.7)	(1,193.5)	(3,002.4)
Score_numeracy	-283.0	-140.8	-151.4	917.8	327.5	388.3	-704.3	-1947.1
	(319.3)	(490.5)	(3,175.3)	(8,159.3)	(602.6)	(1,716.6)	(803.2)	(2,503.1)
Score_financial	901.4	914.9	1269.0	11442.2	-778.7	-878.2	1696.5	900.8
	(579.9)	(897.9)	(2,465.1)	(11,965.8)	(732.1)	(2,176.2)	(1,145.8)	(2,625.7)
Risk preference	-4201.3	3961	-14557.1	-40496.7	21632.1	42940.5	-22936.7	-40702.7
	(7,937.4)	(10,087.2)	(30,945.2)	(121,135.1)	(12,869.2)	(40,443.9)	(15,372.0)	(41,933.6)
Impatience	-5719.3	-4596.7	37819.2	-25739.6	-1170.8	-8537.3	7993.3	21493.6
	(2,996.7)	(4,379.5)	(28,329.5)	(69,138.4)	(4,624.8)	(32,047.0)	(7,517.2)	(18,901.7)
CCEI_risk	1109.8	-531.8	15031.4	53362.9	5988.7	473.1	10994.7	32223.7
	(3,673.3)	(4,596.6)	(19,161.0)	(80,952.1)	(7,554.3)	(15,616.4)	(6,979.6)	(25,306.3)
CCEI_time	4679.5	9336.7	22170.3	-32378.6	-8383.2	-19793.3	3872.8	-7554.3
	(3,723.7)	(6,118.4)	(19,302.3)	(68,956.2)	(7,709.6)	(19,856.0)	(8,384.2)	(20,848.3)
Observation	688	688	125	125	127	127	222	222
TODA fixed effect	No	Yes	No	Yes	No	Yes	No	Yes

continued on next page

Table A1 continued

Panel J	Have borrowed money		Borrowed for property purchase		Borrowed for medical purpose		Borrowed for business operation	
	(1)	(2)	(3)	(4)	(5)	(6)	(7)	(8)
Fintech	-0.119**	-0.146	-0.00344	-0.0207	-0.103**	-0.0968	0.00887	-0.00729
	(0.0319)	(0.0751)	(0.0106)	(0.0189)	(0.0256)	(0.0621)	(0.0121)	(0.0250)
Male	-0.1370	-0.1790	0.0182**	0.0148	-0.1440	-0.1750	-0.0539	-0.0337
	(0.0794)	(0.0958)	(0.0045)	(0.0086)	(0.0854)	(0.0901)	(0.0474)	(0.0509)
Married	0.0717**	0.0819**	0.0152*	0.017	0.0654**	0.0712**	0.0221**	0.0272**
	(0.0269)	(0.0293)	(0.0061)	(0.0088)	(0.0234)	(0.0260)	(0.0068)	(0.0090)
Age	0.0078	0.0099	0.0015	0.0015	-0.0050	-0.0035	0.0008	0.0014
	(0.0061)	(0.0072)	(0.0017)	(0.0019)	(0.0051)	(0.0058)	(0.0017)	(0.0021)
Age2	-0.0002*	-0.0002*	-0.00002	-0.00002	0.00001	0.00000	-0.00001	-0.00002
	(0.00007)	(0.00008)	(0.00002)	(0.00002)	(0.00005)	(0.00006)	(0.00002)	(0.00002)
Exp	0.00397	0.00392	0.00000	-0.00024	0.00373	0.00383	0.00054	0.00116
	(0.00310)	(0.00379)	(0.00082)	(0.00096)	(0.00258)	(0.00306)	(0.00100)	(0.00107)
Exp2	-0.00001	0.00000	0.00000	0.00001	-0.00010	-0.00010	-0.00002	-0.00004
	(0.00008)	(0.00009)	(0.00002)	(0.00002)	(0.00007)	(0.00008)	(0.00002)	(0.00002)
Same province	0.0537*	0.0402	0.0034	0.0034	0.0493**	0.0331	0.0137	0.0196*
	(0.0209)	(0.0237)	(0.0065)	(0.0078)	(0.0185)	(0.0234)	(0.0070)	(0.0096)
Health	0.0285*	0.0269*	-0.0068	-0.0032	0.0182	0.0168	0.0008	-0.0003
	(0.0132)	(0.0132)	(0.0035)	(0.0045)	(0.0117)	(0.0125)	(0.0043)	(0.0048)
HH member	-0.00224	-0.00322	-0.00207	-0.00186	0.00807*	0.00879	0.00178	0.00219
	(0.00484)	(0.00537)	(0.00145)	(0.00159)	(0.00410)	(0.00456)	(0.00164)	(0.00172)
Education	-0.0133**	-0.0125**	-0.0018	-0.0018	-0.00650*	-0.00488	0.00101	0.00116
	(0.00360)	(0.00405)	(0.00102)	(0.00118)	(0.00317)	(0.00372)	(0.00151)	(0.00170)
Training	0.0040	-0.0079	-0.0010	-0.0034	-0.0059	-0.013	0.0059	-0.0024
	(0.0251)	(0.0282)	(0.0070)	(0.0077)	(0.0217)	(0.0261)	(0.0093)	(0.0102)
Motivation	-0.0048	-0.0045	-0.0052	-0.0050	-0.0154	-0.0093	0.0038	0.0055
	(0.0169)	(0.0193)	(0.0047)	(0.0053)	(0.0147)	(0.0171)	(0.0055)	(0.0065)
Past job	0.0605	0.0629	0.0211**	0.0197**	0.0226	0.0195	0.0073	0.0161
	(0.0388)	(0.0443)	(0.0038)	(0.0048)	(0.0333)	(0.0368)	(0.0130)	(0.0152)
Second job	-0.0189	-0.0246	0.0235*	0.0200	0.0164	0.0323	-0.0106	-0.0138
	(0.0279)	(0.0321)	(0.0105)	(0.0109)	(0.0250)	(0.0284)	(0.0097)	(0.0105)
Score_raven	0.0116	0.0112	-0.00727**	-0.00706**	0.0004	0.0039	0.0042	0.0056
	(0.0087)	(0.0106)	(0.0024)	(0.0024)	(0.0080)	(0.0092)	(0.0033)	(0.0036)
Score_numeracy	0.0065	0.0070	0.0008	0.0021	0.0027	0.0030	-0.0007	0.0005
	(0.0060)	(0.0066)	(0.0015)	(0.0015)	(0.0052)	(0.0056)	(0.0020)	(0.0024)
Score_financial	0.0137	0.0069	0.00500*	0.00619**	-0.0095	-0.0124	-0.0012	-0.0021
	(0.0076)	(0.0088)	(0.0022)	(0.0023)	(0.0066)	(0.0080)	(0.0027)	(0.0029)
Risk preference	-0.1150	-0.1330	0.0527	0.0391	0.0720	0.1010	0.0584	0.0768
	(0.1220)	(0.1330)	(0.0313)	(0.0365)	(0.1100)	(0.1160)	(0.0451)	(0.0519)
Impatience	-0.126*	-0.1090	0.0105	0.0028	-0.0711	-0.0534	0.0087	0.0086
	(0.0501)	(0.0582)	(0.0155)	(0.0150)	(0.0442)	(0.0510)	(0.0152)	(0.0171)
CCEI_risk	0.0350	0.0452	0.0012	0.0030	-0.0621	-0.0767	-0.0142	-0.0177
	(0.0605)	(0.0664)	(0.0144)	(0.0178)	(0.0547)	(0.0673)	(0.0216)	(0.0251)
CCEI_time	-0.1310	-0.0986	0.0058	-0.0022	-0.0760	-0.0128	-0.0062	0.0052
	(0.0731)	(0.0846)	(0.0177)	(0.0187)	(0.0677)	(0.0715)	(0.0266)	(0.0281)
Observation	2,474	2,474	2,474	2,474	2,474	2,474	2,474	2,474
TODA fixed effect	No	Yes	No	Yes	No	Yes	No	Yes

CCEI = Critical Cost Efficiency Index, HH = household, TODA = tricycle operators and drivers' association.

Note: The table shows estimation result of the impact of fintech loan on drivers' welfare, financial planning, and financial accessibility. The independent variable of interest is a fintech dummy indicating whether one has availed of fintech loan. Odd-numbered columns do not include TODA fixed effect terms, and even-numbered columns include them. Standard errors are reported in parentheses. For estimation with TODA fixed effect, standard errors are clustered at TODA level. ** and * represent 5% and 1% significance, respectively.

Source: Asian Development Bank.